That's Life

If I seem like an idiot, that's probably because I am

Chris Philippe Hemingway

Copyright © 2019 Chris Philippe Hemingway

All rights reserved.

ISBN: 9781689930963

DEDICATION

I want to thank my best mate Norman for forcing me into writing this book! Special thanks to my lovely wife for reading the book and still loving me. And also, great appreciation to my friends who supported me with their great feedback; Mark, Adam, Lee, Matt, Conor, Danny, Prabhu, Will, Michael, Tudorel. I wish you the most precious thing I can think of: may these stories never happen to you!

CHAPTERS

The SMS 1

The Man 9

The Brownie 13

The Orchestra 19

The Prompter 23

The Dam 28

The Church 34

The Knee 39

The Cat Litter 47

The Award 51

The Graduation Ceremony 56

Violent Brittany 64

The French Wind 69

The Explanation 73

The Army General 77

The Keychain 83

The Bus 88

Eric 95

The Chocolate Cake 101

The Airplane 106

That's Life

The SMS

Owning your own business comes with a lot of responsibility. It doesn't matter if it is big or small. If you have a business of your own, you often find that you have to frequently rely on other people, customers, or clients in particular. This is one of the reasons why it requires such a great dedication to succeed. I was lucky enough to gather enough money at one point in my life that I was able to start my own business, and I found myself to be even luckier when it was successful. One part was that it was really hard work, and the other part was luck. But I guess luck is a stranger to my life that likes to appear at the most unexpected moment and leave just as quickly, and randomly I might add, as she showed up.

One day one of the biggest music composers in Hungary asked me to work with him. He was close to seventy already, and he had earned quite a bit of respect from everyone around him since almost everyone knows his name in my country. In this story, I am just going to call him "Mr C," not to give away his identity. He was the kind of guy you wanted to work with and impress, so that you could put it on your CV, to impress everyone else with it. Everyone admires Mr C, and if you are working with him, then people will think that you must be very good at what you do.

He was about to give a big concert at one of Budapest's greatest music halls, and my responsibility, as well as my crew's, was to shoot a video of the whole thing. It is not an easy process, and you definitely don't want to screw it up.

That is why I was so shocked that beautiful Friday morning in the summer, as I sat on the toilet, and realised that I had accidentally made a huge mistake.

I was still working as an actor at the time, and matinee shows start at 10 AM sharp as kids are escorted there from school by their teachers. In this show, I played one of the main roles, and because it involved singing and dancing, I had to wake up as early as possible to warm up. Then, I usually had to arrive two hours before the show to dress up in costume, and let the sound engineers do some sound checking with my face mic, while I do some singing on stage for them.

The whole day started, though, with me sitting on the toilet, just after I woke up. In the weeks before this, I asked my wife several times to fix the toilet seat, as it was constantly moving sideways. As funny as this sounds, she is the better handyman out of the two of us. She has a great talent for fixing anything which is physically broken. So, I often find myself telling people if there is a software issue, I'm fixing it, and if there is a hardware issue, I call on Laura. It just so happened that at this time, the toilet seat was still very easily moveable. So after about a minute or so of me sitting there, I had begun to slide sideways, and before I knew it in my customary catatonic state of mind at that time in the morning, I had fallen off the toilet completely. I was sitting on the floor like an idiot, and though it took me a few seconds to figure out what had happened, I found the situation to be quite funny. After I proceeded to clean myself up and resumed my seat atop the toilet, I immediately wrote a message to my best mate to tell him what had happened. This is just something we have done for a long time now. When we have free time, we either write to one another if something funny has happened or occasionally to make things a little more fun, we write a brief poem of the story. Then we send it to each other that way, and, this is exactly what happened here. Except, I didn't send it to him. As shameful as it is, my mate's first name is quite close in the alphabet to the composer's name who I was about to work for.

After sending the poem as an SMS, I hadn't really realised at first that I sent it to the wrong person. Once I discovered what had happened, I could only imagine the look on the wrinkled face of the old respected chap who was reading this on a Friday morning, in an unexpected SMS from his director of videography, only one day before his big concert. I could also only imagine that he most likely thought that I was referring to his show in the poem, while I was indeed talking about the one which I was about to be in that morning. So, without further ado, here is the poem.

The show will start soon, and we're almost there,
So I meet the toilet, that's just fair.
I'm half-dreaming as I hail the poop,
Chris hopes that it all goes down the loo.

That's Life

I'm sitting there like the king on the throne
My noble part is filling the big hole.
I'm waiting there like others for the gold,
But the toilet seat is fairly cold.

Here we are, I feel we're almost there.
The poop comes out like dragon from the lair.
Once it's out, I'm calling it a truce,
though the toilet seat is fairly loose.

Actually, it's so bad that it moves,
I slide aside and sound just like a goose.
I'm falling quickly hearing a weird sound
as my dirty butt touches the ground.

Let's just clean the mess and go away,
My fate is the predator, I'm the prey.
It's time for me to stand up and then glow,
I think I am now ready for the show.

For the better part of a few moments, I was really glad as I read the SMS back to myself, very proud and happy at the result. Then, suddenly, the phone said, "Read."

"Great," I thought. "I am sure he will have a good laugh." Then I looked at the top of the screen and suddenly became very confused and slightly horrified. The name was Mr C, not my mate. In a scenario like this, my brain usually reacts by trying to deny reality, as I remember not believing right away that what my phone was telling me the truth. I remembered I had selected the right name, so for it to be telling me what it was telling me couldn't be right. Or could it? It took several minutes for me to slowly digest everything that was going on and the fact that I had indeed sent the message to the wrong person. I literally froze in terror and couldn't believe that I had done such a thing. This time, I read through the poem once again, but in a panic, trying to make sure that there was nothing in its contents of which I would be ashamed of. Upon reaching the second line, I had to stop myself. I covered my face with both of my hands, in utter shame, and I sat there for several minutes as the feelings washed over me. "This isn't happening," I told myself, hoping that somehow it would make it true and that the situation would listen and go away.

  This was back when it was early days yet for smartphones to be out, but both he and I had the same type of phone; which were already using wi-fi for messages whenever it was available. They had a feature not only to show when the message had been read, but also when the other person was typing. So, when I saw him begin to type, I got really scared. "What the hell is he going to say?" Then after about ten seconds, he stopped. And, both to my relief as well as dismay, he never responded.

  After finishing with the early morning show, I told the story to my friends and colleagues, who all responded by laughing so hard that they cried. This was probably the first time that anyone ever suggested that I start writing my stories down. Although, I didn't care about that at the moment as I was in a very serious mood about the whole thing, and felt ashamed of myself. So, I simply asked them to give me advice on what I should do next. They all, however, did agree on one thing. I should call Mr C and speak to him about what happened, and I needed to apologise. Even though I knew they were right, it wasn't the kind of conversation anyone would expect to have with this kind of person. But unfortunately, it was inevitable.

So I waited an entire day before ringing him up the next morning. I knew this conversation could only go one of two ways. He could either think about it humorously and maybe ask me if I had any other story for today, or he could be dead serious. And, when he answered the phone, he sounded dead serious.

"Mr C, sorry for bothering you," I began. "I wondered if you had the chance to read the message I sent you yesterday morning." This was followed by him being silent for what seemed like an eternity as I waited for him to respond. Then, suddenly, he changed his tone and asked, "What message are you referring to exactly?"

"Are you kidding me?" I thought. "Is he joking, or is he expecting me to read out the full poem to him?" I was utterly confused, as I saw my phone clearly showing me that he had read the message. Even though I now realise that this could also mean that a person just opened the message without glancing at it at all, before closing it or deleting it. This logic was something I definitely could have used at that moment to calm myself, but my mind was too frantic with social anxiety and the awkwardness of the situation to process that kind of intelligent thought. "Well," I stuttered a bit as I do when I get nervous. "I must have sent a silly message, but to be honest it wasn't meant to be sent to you, but for my best mate. My phone is quite new, and I still haven't gotten used to it, and sometimes, very rarely, I send the messages to the wrong person, so--"

"Chris, let me stop you there." He interrupted. His voice was now calm, and it even sounded like he was smiling. "Don't worry about it at all. Let's just agree that I have absolutely no idea what message you are talking about, and I am looking forward to working with you today at the concert."

It was one of the greatest reliefs of my life. "What an intelligent gentleman." I thought, and what an elegant way to end my misery, which had laid like a burden on me the entire day before.

Suddenly, I realised that becoming a big man in something is not just about being talented in what you do. It is the permanent and genuine respect that you get from other people around you, which comes from the fact that you are understanding and respectful to them. You make it clear that you are not that different from them, and you handle others with the same amount of respect with which you expect to be treated. Do unto others as you would have them do unto you, it says it for a reason, folks. Last but most certainly not least, having a healthy sense of humour is important, too. This was a lesson that I learned very well from my experience with Mr C.

To be honest, almost a decade has passed since this story took place, and I am now living in another country, doing a completely different job. But still, I occasionally catch myself wondering about giving Mr C a call, asking him how he is doing nowadays, and then ask him the question that has still been weighing on my mind for quite some time now.

"Mr C, how did you like my poem?"

The Man

Stories are a big part of our lives. Everything that happens to us, even if it only happens once, becomes a part of the great tapestry of the story that is our life. And, depending on the nature of the story, we tend to split them into smaller threads and organise them according to how we think they should best be arranged. Much like how a person would format a novel's flow, we decide which ones are best to share with our close friends, our families, or the world.

It is a clear and present fact that people much prefer to share the ones which they can put a positive spin on. As human beings, we have a tendency not to feel too comfortable sharing those stories which put us in a harsh light. The stories that feature us as the object of humiliation or as the person who made the wrong decision in any given situation. I, in many ways, used to be the same way. Having grown to be the person I am today, shaped by such stories, will be the first to admit this. All the bad things that have happened to me I tried to keep to myself, to bury them so deeply that maybe even I could convince myself to one day see them differently than they were. Or perhaps even forget them altogether. But for some reason, the deeper I seemed to bury them, the more often I found myself in similar situations. And, as anyone who understands the law of attraction, knowing that like attracts like. The further you put something into your subconscious, the more power it is given. Which caused me to wonder if there might be some lesson to be learned here, and that life was trying to teach me that I needed to learn to deal with these situations head-on rather than run from them.

So, as with most things in my life, I tried to begin by looking at them through the prism of humour. This gave me the strength to view many of these situations and happenings in a different light. In turn, it caused me to become more comfortable and accepting of the tapestry that they were creating. Therefore, giving me the peace of mind to share them with my friends. Much to my surprise and delight, it quickly turned out that as much as I was ashamed of these stories, in the beginning, the reaction that I received to them was very welcoming. So, I decided to share them with the rest of the world, thus, freeing myself from this burden of trying to stuff them deep into the recesses of my mind, giving me the clarity that I so desperately needed to understand. These stories of mine could serve as examples to others on how NOT to behave in certain situations, and also providing people with a little humour along the way. Which we all know everyone could use a little more of that in their life.

I suppose this curse, of getting myself into funny and uncomfortable situations began before I was born. So, I guess you could say that it is somewhat of a family curse. Though I was born and raised in Budapest, Hungary, my family is originally from Austria, and some of them are from Germany. We were living with my great grandparents in a flat for many years in Budapest, and during this time, my great-grandfather had the opportunity to share a lot of stories of his own with me. The majority of these stories, of course, were about the first and second World War. How important it is to learn from history in order to become better men. For it is through the study of history that we can help ourselves and the future generations who are willing to listen not to repeat the same mistakes. At least we hope not. This is why he always wanted me to learn how important it is to be kind, as well as precise from as early of an age as possible. Even though in some aspects of the kind part, I as most human beings have failed always to be so. For with one, sometimes you must sacrifice the other, however, mistakenly that train of thought. Thus, it is a sad commentary of humanity.

My great-grandfather was a wonderful, truly great man, with a lot of values. But I always thought of him as a serious and strict sort of man, who only ever smiled; yet never truly laughed. This thought was very difficult for me to attune to a story I heard many years after he had passed away, and I am sure this must have caused a hell of a moment for him. The other thing that amazed me was the fact it was a story that involved my great-grandfather that had nothing to do with one of the wars.

My uncle told me that during the '60s my great grandparents went for a family visit in Hamburg, Germany to see relatives who they saw only every two to three years or so. The visit went very well, and they were having a nice dinner made by the lady of the house. They also had a nice conversation about how things were going in Hungary, and how the business seemed to be going better those days. At some point in the evening, my great-grandfather, Carl, excused himself to go to the bathroom.

He spent the better part of five minutes in there before returning to the table to continue the conversation. A few moments later, the lady of the house went away from the table and came back shortly after. She stood right in the doorway, her face filled with panic. Then, out of nowhere, she expressed the concern that was written all over her face to my great-grandmother. Telling her, with anxiety coating her voice, "Oh my dear, your husband's poo smells so bad, that I think you should have him checked out by a doctor."

It happened at least thirty years before I was born, but I would have given almost anything to travel back in time if only to see my great-grandfather's face after this uncomfortable announcement. The most precise man I have ever known, with a higher reputation among his friends than I could ever hope to have even in a sliver of my lifetime, in a world where reputation wasn't achieved by the number of likes as it is today, but by the acts and manner in which a person carried with them in their daily lives and defined themselves before the rest of the world.

This story helped me to realise that it does not matter how great or popular you are. No matter your status or place in the world, you are no different from any other men or women anywhere else. You could be the CEO of a multibillion-dollar company, the president of a country, the head of a church, but at the end of the day, we are all not so different from each other. And, even though a good portion of the world believes that theirs does not...all of our shit stinks!

The Brownie

On a beautiful sunny day in August, I decided to go out for a walk on my lunch break. I was planning on doing a big presentation after I got back from my break, so I wanted to make sure that my mind was clear. I thought that taking a nice stroll would do just the trick, and the warm weather in England was much appreciated.

I had the most effortless way to the park. The birds were singing, and the clouds decided not to stand too much in the way of the sun. The conditions were perfect. So naturally, I headed straight for the grass and sat on a bench in the middle of the beautiful green field. The view was spectacular, and the space around me was vast. As I sat there, taking in the peacefulness of the environment around me, I took the vegan brownie that I had brought with me full of dark chocolate by the way, out of my hoodie pocket. Then, I began to eat it, not thinking about the upcoming presentation at all. I was just relaxing and enjoying the beautiful weather.

I was very careful though with the wrapping as I didn't want to directly touch the brownie, for fear of making a mess all over my hands with chocolate like some toddler, just before presenting to the CTO. I rather preferred to use the paper wrapping as a sort of buffer between my dessert and my hand, so that I could stay clean. But unfortunately, as I was about to grab the last bite, the last small piece somehow managed to slip out of my grasp and fall right into the grass.

I have never in my whole life been the kind of person to litter. Never. But because it was just a piece of chocolate, I thought, "What the hell, it's going to decompose anyway, right?"

So I stood up from the bench, turned around, and headed right back to work. During my walk, I noticed pretty much right away that something was not right. I couldn't quite define what exactly was wrong. All I knew was that I had that overwhelming feeling that you usually get when you know that you have forgotten something important, but you can't quite put your finger on it.

By this time, I had almost made it back to the building when the realisation struck me like a bolt of lightning from the sky. "Dogs!" This park was usually full of dogs, and dogs can't eat chocolate, according to many social media posts that I constantly saw online that told me it functioned as some poison when a dog ingests it. I don't have a dog, so, I couldn't be completely certain about this fact. But, I felt that even if there was the slightest chance that this could be true, I shouldn't risk poisoning someone else's dog by leaving a piece of chocolate brownie in the middle of the park.

I turned around, and I began to sprint back to the park, almost like what you would see in one of those action movies, where the hero is trying to prevent a bomb from going off. I glanced on the watch on my wrist to check the time and realised that I could still make it back to give my presentation if I was quick enough to grab the offending chocolate, throw it in the closest bin, and run straight back to work.

So, of course, with most things in life, once life has figured out that it is important for you to get somewhere and accomplish something quickly, it makes it its mission to throw every monkey wrench known to man in your way to prevent you from getting there on time. You get every red light on the crosswalks, every driver imaginable who thinks that they are some race car driver, and right about this time would be the perfect time for all of the trucks to revert to the alleys behind the shops. Thus, blocking the closest possible route back to the park. Every second felt like the longest minute of my life as I was already envisioning in my mind's eyes, some poor defenceless dog picking up the chocolate, freezing suddenly and falling over on its side. All the while pointing an accusatory paw at me, like Joffrey pointed at Tyrion after being poisoned at his wedding.

The anxiety was just terrible. "I would never harm a dog." I thought to myself, trying to pick up my speed.

Finally, I reached the park, and luckily enough, I saw only one little English Cocker Spaniel with his owner, strolling along the grass. The chap must have at least been in his seventies. Obviously, the kind of person who has already retired and like spending his afternoons leisurely walking through the park with his dog, while enjoying the view.

I went back to the bench and started looking for the brownie. The fact that the grass had not been cut recently did not help the situation at all. "It must be here," I thought frantically to myself. "I know I dropped it right here."

The dog suddenly came up to me with the usual look on his face. The one that tells you to pet him a little bit just to become friends, even if only for the moment. If I haven't said it already, or you haven't noticed by now, I love dogs. I love the uncontrolled unconditional love, affection, and trust they can present to even a complete stranger. And though I found it cute that he came to me, I quickly realised that this was probably the worst possible moment for me to be around a dog right now, as I was still looking for the chocolate. It was almost as if the dog heard my thoughts because he quickly discovered that I was onto something, and started sniffing around in the grass in a more excited state.

"For God's sake," I thought as I glanced up at the elderly owner who was only 30 meters away, getting closer and closer to us. "The dog is going to find it before me. He is going to die because of me. And, then, this nice chap is going to have a heart attack when his dog passes out, and they both are going to die because of me." This train of thought utterly upset and distressed me. By now, I was sweating like a snowman in the middle of summer, and nearly on all fours myself next to the dog. I was searching frantically, realising with every passing moment that there was no way that I was going to find it sooner than this sniffing machine with a million times more smelling power than I could ever wish to have. I nearly gave up, when suddenly out of nowhere, I saw it. It was like a meter away.

"How the hell did it fall that far?" I exclaimed to myself. It didn't matter, all that mattered right then was that I reached out, grabbed it, and could finally straighten up to a standing position, knowing that I had rescued the dog and the man from certain death.

The feeling of euphoric accomplishment was like reaching the gates of Heaven. I had a long tiring journey to get there, but I had finally made it. There was nothing which could have ruined this holy moment for me, or at least I thought so until I heard the old man say, "What was that?" I didn't quite catch it at first as I was still basking in the shining glory of my triumph that was still pumping up my ego. He was only about 10 meters away when he waved at me again and kindly shouted to me. "Don't worry about that. I'll handle it."

I was a little confused. First of all, how in the hell did he know that there was a piece of leftover brownie in the grass? He couldn't have seen me when I was here before, could he? Also, even if he knew about it, why would he be the one to handle it? After all, it was my brownie, my responsibility. I was the guilty party, the one at fault in this. So I tried to take on the most serious, responsible looking, face I could muster, and while I waved at him with the brownie in my bare hand, and I kindly shouted back. "No way, don't worry about it, It belongs to me,"

To this day, I will never forget the look on the man's face, probably until the day I die. He was completely befuddled. The expression of confusion on his face was overwhelming as well as mingled with something I could only describe later as disgust when I finally realised the truth, of course. However, at that time, I was still unaware of what was going on. I turned around and headed out of the park, marching purposefully back to my work-place. I was trying to get back as quickly as possible. Meanwhile, my head became suddenly filled with an ocean of different thoughts.

I was holding my vegan brownie in my right hand like some trophy, not having the smallest clue about why a stranger would want to take responsibility for a piece of chocolate that I had dropped in the grass. What did he even mean by, 'he would handle it'? Shouldn't he be more worried about taking care of his dog?

Then suddenly, I realised: "Oh, shit."

The Orchestra

One phrase that I grew up hearing a lot was, "If you don't know anyone weirder than you, there is a good chance you are the weirdest person around." This proverb has never filled me with much courage, as I rarely come across anyone, I have ever considered being odder than I. This, however, has its advantages too. I am, for the most part, great with people. I can usually relate to almost anyone, and I make a great partner for conversation almost all the time. On the other hand, leave me to my own devices for a few minutes or a few seconds, and I will somehow find a way to embarrass myself.

I was sitting at my work desk with the new laptop I had gotten from the company to work on. Back in that workplace, there were no designated desks for particular people. There were too many people working for the company as contractors. So, everything was pretty much an "if a desk is free, you can use it today" kind of environment. I remember it was autumn, and for some reason, British people like to leave the AC on in their offices right up until winter arrives, so I was wrapped up in my hoodie and scarf, feeling like someone who was about to freeze to death. I was very deep into my work, but familiarising myself with the new machine held me back a bit with the continuous coding.

All of a sudden, I heard the sound of a trumpet. The sound came from very far away, it was almost non-existent, but I could tell it was there. I played the trumpet myself for eight years and is one of my favourite instruments, and I never fail to recognise it when I hear it played in a band. This time it was a bit different though. No other instruments were playing, just this one in solo. It took a few seconds longer before it stopped.

"It must have come from the street." I thought to myself, but I still found it weird as our workplace was located very close to a forest, with no frequent visitors around the building. So, I got back to work. But a few seconds later, the trumpet began to blow again. This time it was coming from much closer, and clearer, too. I had a suspicion that someone may have brought a trumpet to the workplace and was now showing off to the others. I wouldn't have been surprised at that, as I saw people showing up previously with their dogs and their children, so a trumpet would not have necessarily been an odd thing to add to the list.

I must have looked too curious watching my back, searching for the source of the sound as another person, who I had never seen before, seated on my left began to look at me with curiosity, as well. I didn't want him to think I was crazy, so I turned to him a bit and kindly said:
"This is great. It's hard to blow it like that." Just then, I felt I must have said something wrong because the guy looked back at me with a very confused expression on his face. "He has no idea," I thought to myself. But that's okay, not everyone is a fan of music, and I totally get that. I just smiled and looked around to check if anyone else was enjoying the sound of the instrument as I did. The more I looked, the more people looked back at me with curiosity.

"Now they start to get it."

Genuinely, though, it is really hard to blow a trumpet in a way that sounds as clear as it did back at that moment. Whoever played it, it was clear to me that he was no amateur. Though, if it is someone who works here, he must have changed professions. Not a big deal, I had changed professions as well to become an engineer. These things happen.

My thoughts started to race and immediately took me into a world where I was trying to figure out how the trumpet player ended up here at this company. Since the sound still came from a bit further away, and no one behind me seemed to be playing, it was quite clear that it was someone from the first floor where the finance department was located. Interesting. I knew many musicians who had civil jobs, but no one who would actually-- suddenly, before I could finish my thought. BAM! Within a millisecond, the loud blast of an orchestra playing resounded in my ears, scaring me half to death and causing me to jump up from my office chair. I felt as if I was going to go deaf immediately, hearing dozens of instruments giving the biggest introductory sounds together, ever known to man. Without a doubt, it was a proper symphonic orchestra, complete with bass drums and cymbals.

I honestly felt as if someone had kicked me in the back and knocked the wind out of me — a surprise attack with no warning whatsoever. I suppose the movement of my hands was as instinctual of action as leaping from the chair, trying to cover my ears to buffer them against the very loud and sudden music. After I had leaped from the chair, reaching my hands to my ears is what helped me to realise what exactly was happening.

This was the first day I had ever used wireless earphones in my entire life. I had only just gotten these the day before, setting them up with the new laptop I had gotten that morning, and then I proceeded to forget about them for the next several hours. I can only guess what might have happened was that I had pushed a wrong button on the new type of keyboard, which triggered some classical music in the background at maximum volume.

I slowly gathered the puzzle pieces together one by one as I was standing there next to my desk, and in the meantime, I quickly took out the earbuds. My pulse was racing so quickly. I could hear the pounding of my heart in my ears. Finally, I looked around slowly and noticed that my jump had pushed the table and caused a bit of a chain reaction with the other's work desks around me. So, people were now staring at me with terror in their eyes.

"Should I explain?" I asked myself, but I decided to go to the loo instead. As I departed the huge open space behind me as I walked out, there was only one thought that came to mind.

"If you don't know anyone weirder than you, there is a good chance you are the weirdest person around."

The Prompter

When I was a stage actor, we used to watch our shows from the outside whenever we had the chance. It's one thing to play in it, but when you have a day off, and someone else plays your character, you either rest at home or go back to the theatre and watch how the other guy plays your role. One benefit of working for a theatre is that you never have to pay to watch any shows. This is a great opportunity to learn things from others, as acting is a never-ending process, and you can only get better at it if you watch others, and how they do it. There might be slight things which the actor does differently, and you definitely don't want to copy him, but it's always the best place to get inspiration when you see other's different vision on how to bring your character to life.

If I had a time machine, I would probably go back to watch a certain show in the early 2000s which I unfortunately missed, and which has become so famous on its own, that it became part of the most famous theatre stories ever in the country. They played Romeo and Juliet, and it's not an exaggeration to say that the prompter of the show that night (who I will now call Melanie to protect her real identity) literally took a step up in her job, causing a chain of events that changed Shakespeare's play in ways no one would ever perceive possible.

It all started with the dagger of Paris, the chap who is fully in love with Juliet and is ready to fight with Romeo at the crypt as it's played on stage. The dagger is, of course, not sharp, but just for the record, it is still reasonably heavy. It is just like a real dagger, made of metal, as it needs to look as real as possible. In this particular show, the dagger fell out of the hands of Gabriel, the actor who played Paris during their fight scene. But that's alright, these things happen, and they are actors for a reason. Improvising may not be the most efficient thing to do when playing Shakespeare, but clearly doable, and that's just the magic of a live show. Glorious spontaneity.

However, Melanie didn't think of it that way. Her duty was basically to whisper the lines to the ones on stage whenever it was necessary, and that's pretty much it. But that night she couldn't help but notice that the dagger was on the ground, and the guys were still fighting. She didn't assume the actors could solve this issue on their own, and therefore, probably for the first time in the Hungarian Theatre History, as a responsible prompter, someone who cares for the show, she thought it best to intervene.

According to the people in the audience, the first thing they noticed in the first few rows was her voice. Melanie started shouting in a whispering tone with a moderate volume to the actors. "The dagger. The dagger is on the floor."

I had the chance to talk to the guys playing that particular night, and according to them they heard the prompter's voice, and they almost started to repeat back the words, as they thought they left something out from their speech. By the time they realised what Melanie was talking about, they started to send furious looks in the direction where she was sitting on her chair, to let her know they were just fine. But Melanie didn't get the idea. In the next few moments, the thousand people in the audience were able to watch a hand at the left of the stage, grab the black drape which covers the left-wing of the stage. We call that narrow curtain a "leg." Melanie went on all fours, and grabbed the drape from the inside, leaving her fingers visible to the audience, and then started to move slowly to the centre of the stage, pulling the leg with her which was covering more and more are of the stage. She was moving forward slowly, and in 10 seconds, she reached the point where the dagger was laying. At this point she reached out, making her entire arm and shoulders visible, and took the dagger. According to my friends, who were among the rows of audience members, they didn't understand what was happening, as Melanie was about to go back on the floor, slowly to the direction she came from.

Finally, she had the dagger in her hands. "Gabriel!" she whispered very loudly to the actor who was playing Paris. "The dagger. I have the dagger. It's here."
Gabriel, of course, was still trying to act, as well as fight with Romeo, and they eventually made their way to the location where Gabriel planned to take up his weapon. Except his weapon wasn't there anymore. He got very confused. I can only imagine his face as he slowly turned to the left-wing/backstage area, looking for answers, but not too long, so the audience didn't notice that he was looking for something. Melanie, on the other hand, was really happy, as she was swinging the weapon in the air backstage so that Gabriel could see it.

You would imagine by now, someone needed to do something to solve this issue, but the audience was frozen completely taken aback by what they were witnessing. The staff in the backstage were shocked, and even the actor who played Romeo did hold his breath.

"So, What are you going to do now?" he shouted to Paris on stage very convincingly, staying in character. "You can't kill me."

"I can kill you with my bare hands, you bastard!" he responded, perfectly-staying in character, and he started to accelerate to catch his nemesis.

That was the ultimate moment for Melanie. She prepared the weapon, pulled it up above her head, behind her shoulders, aimed, and threw it to the stage to save the show.

"Here's the knife!" she whispered very loudly.

Melanie might not have been the best problem solver, but as it turns out, she was a wonderful thrower of daggers. The weapon was rotating in the air for several seconds it seemed, making its way to the stage like an arrow which was just shot out from a bow. It came from the left side of the stage, sailing across everyone's eyes, and then perfectly hitting Paris in the back of his head, who then fell to the stage.

Well, it's true to say Paris needed to die in this scene, but this implementation of the play was clearly outstanding, and never seen before. People were shocked, and even Romeo didn't know what to do. Luckily enough, the actor wasn't seriously harmed, and since everyone liked Melanie, she also only got away with a warning from the director of the theatre, after the show.

She promised that she would never enter the stage ever again, and just in case they made an explicit regulation in the theatre which became legendary: a prompter can never step on the stage during playtime.

The Dam

We were working late at the studio one evening, dubbing one of the newest movies which were coming ready for release. And, though I knew the sound engineer quite well, I wanted to get on well with the audio director, too. This was because this was my first time working with him, and I wanted to make a good impression. Because, really and honestly, first impressions and your reputation are everything in this business.

He was quite a severe sort of guy. The only thing that denoted him as not being too serious was the fact he had a habit of whistling. I have never understood the point of whistling, especially when it is entirely random, out of nowhere, and not even a complete song. I mean, come on! To me, it is like starting to sing random notes and lyrics from a song in the middle of a crowded bus. And, I am pretty sure this behaviour would inspire everyone around me to turn and look at me like I had five or six heads. Then, I would be labelled for sure as a crazy person. But if you whistle random things, instead, that counts as completely normal behaviour that is accepted by everyone. It's weird, but whatever.

Anyway, we were in the process of completing our recording session, when we were finally given a 10-minute break; after working for three or four hours straight without one. So, I headed to the toilet, as one usually does when you are given a break after a long period of work. There was something different about this time than the others. For some reason, which remains unclear to me to this day, I was hit with the overwhelming urge to throw up. This caused me to make my way to the toilet with great urgency, as I didn't want to blow chunks somewhere other than the bathroom and humiliate myself in front of the sound director; whom, I so desperately desired to impress.

I am not entirely sure whether the sick feeling was from food poisoning due to something I had eaten earlier on in the day, or if it was merely the fact I was nervous about impressing the director. But all I knew at that moment for sure was that a storm was brewing inside of me that was about to release a volcanic eruption, and it was going to come out somehow; which end I couldn't be certain. So, I made haste to the bathroom.

When I finally made it to the toilet, after what seemed like an eternity, I realised to my horror that there were only two stalls in the bathroom, and one of them was already occupied. My first thought was, "Shit, this sucks." Because I cannot stand the thought of other people listening when I am trying to relieve myself from either orifice and, when you are not feeling right there are obviously things to listen to, am I right?

So, anyway, without going into too much gory detail; all I can say is that what happened next can almost be compared to a magnificent orchestral piece that didn't stop for the better part of five minutes. Suffice it to say. I had the worst diarrhoea, ever. I felt right in that moment it was the worst case in the history of humankind, and somehow it had been bestowed upon me, just then. Damn, how lucky am I?

For moments I wondered about the other guy in the neighbouring stall, and when he would become bored or uncomfortable and leave. During the pauses of the grand orchestra that was playing, where my ass bassoon was the star, I heard tranquil music and the sound of talking, which made me realise, to my somewhat relief, that he was most likely watching a movie on his phone. And, this is why he probably didn't care about the inglorious chorus being carried on by my behind in the stall next to him. "Thank god," I thought.

Well, after I finally finished, I thought to myself, "let's get the hell out of here." I only had a few minutes left from our break interval anyway. But when I flushed the toilet, my worst possible nightmare came to life before my very eyes. I watched as the brown water rose higher and higher in the bowl. It is always a scary thing to watch, even when you are at home, much less in public, and much worse at work. But when this does happen most of the time, it just goes back after a while, and you breathe a big sigh of relief, which is precisely what you would expect to feel in the toilet.

However, not this time, though. The muddy fluid rose higher and higher until it reached a critical point. The ceramic border which is meant for the sole purpose of holding those demons which are never supposed to leave the underworld back. Once the edge was passed, I knew there was no going back. We had indeed reached the point of no return. This sentiment was even more compounded when I tried in one last-ditch effort to flush the toilet once again to see if perhaps that would set the cycle to rights. But all of my hopes were dashed when suddenly the handle seemed to disintegrate in my hands completely. I stood there for the longest time staring at the broken pieces. After this, my first immediate thought was to quickly flee the scene, when suddenly that familiar disjointed whistling hit my ears as someone entered the toilet. I waited with bated breath as my mind flashed, "It's him, right at the worst possible moment." I truly am the luckiest guy in the world, don't you know?

Well, there was a reasonable gap between the ground and the outer world beyond the stall, also another one between the two cabins in which the guy was still watching his show.

"What do I do now?" I wondered, doing my best not to panic. Because you never think very clearly when you panic. But I was well past that point. Do not pass calm, do not collect two hundred, if you know what I mean?

I had recognised the whistling, and I knew that I didn't want the director to see my watered faeces floating around the stall floor. So, I responded to the situation with the only thing that made sense to me at the time. Why, build a dam of toilet paper, of course!

I took the toilet paper canister from the wall, which luckily was a huge one with multiple rolls inside, and I started to roll out as much paper as I possibly could in the shortest amount of time. I had two goals in mind, at this point. One, to cover the gap shared with the outside world. Two, to cover the space in the wall which was shared by the adjacent stall. After all, I didn't want to surprise my neighbour in the other booth with something creeping out from below.

We all know those scenes from those horror movies in which the blood flows out of from under the stalls, alerting the other players to someone's unfortunate demise. And, I am quite sure that it would be equally as shocking to have muddy, watery shit creating the same effect. Not to mention, it would most likely be met with quite the same, if not, somewhat similar reaction. So, this is why I started to build my dam.

I didn't want to build it right under the gap, as anyone would have been able to see it from the outside what I was doing. So, I crammed the small space into an even smaller rectangle and began to lay down the layers of paper one by one.

In the meantime, I didn't seem to notice that the water flow from the toilet in my stall was not coming to a stop. So even though for a few seconds, the whole structure I was building had a promising beginning, the new waves of water and shit started to destroy everything as quickly as I could construct it. The paper absorbed the water like a sponge, which is what it was designed to do, but of course, I was not thinking about that at the time. It became soft and mushy, making my entire fortress less and less reliable.

At this point, I was on the verge of tears, covered in sweat, and shitty water. The water slowly continued to rise, and even though I still had some paper left to work with, the reality was that I was standing in the middle of a pool. A pool of my feces and it stunk to high heaven.

It felt like an eternity in hell for me, continuing to build my ever-growing dam, and I knew it was only a matter of time before the others would decide to leave. Which eventually happened. I almost couldn't believe it, when I heard the door opening, and him leaving the other guy to go in. I only had to wait until he washed his hands, dried them, and finally vacated the loo.

When I finally was released from my shitty cage, I turned back for a second to look upon the massacre that had rendered this bathroom stall nearly unrecognisable. It was even worse than I could have imagined while I was trapped inside of it, building my dam. And, I knew that I was only seconds away from the sound director finding out about this little fiasco from the other cabin. I knew I had to leave, and I had to leave quickly. But for a split second, I gave some serious consideration to reporting it to someone, and then I realised there was no way that news of this wouldn't make it around the building in a matter of minutes without me intervening. It took me a few minutes to calm myself down and act like a normal human being.

Finally, I calmed myself enough to make a report to the staff as someone who "just happened to see" that the toilet was acting weird. I have tried for many years to bury this memory and bury it deep. I only talked to a friend of mine about it when it happened. Now that years have passed, I can now think about it humorously. Even though, sometimes I find myself wondering about what the look must have been on the face of the poor staff, who entered after I left the scene of the crime. I wonder what they must have thought about the fortress I had built, the dam of toilet paper that I had created. I can't even begin to imagine.

The Church

There is nothing funnier than seeing someone in an awkward situation who you wouldn't ever usually imagine being in one. I suppose that's why some jokes are more powerful when a subject is a famous person like the president or the Pope. People you would never expect to get themselves into that kind of trouble. And, that's also true of my father, who is a serious man by all reports. Most certainly not the type who likes to be seen as the goofy one, but even he went too far once.

I must have been about eight years old at the time, when we went for a field trip with my parents and my sister, to visit some famous town in the North-East area of Hungary. The journey was long but was definitely worth it. We saw some amazing places and wild animal in the fields that we passed.

When it started to get late, we headed back to the capital, but along the way, we drove through a little village called "Perkupa." We had never been there before, but my father, as proud of his family as he is, suddenly remembered this village's name to be one who was home to his grandfather. My great-grandfather did not just live here, to be honest, but he was so influential in this small village that everyone knew him or at least knew of him. He was the one who financed the church to be built in the centre of the village, and for that, he was always remembered there. My grandmother was always telling stories about him, how lovely of a man he was, and especially how popular he was back in the day.

This was clearly our time to shine, and my father also clearly saw it as an opportunity to stop for a little bit just next to the small church and tell us about all of the great things our great-grandfather had done there. Interestingly enough, the local pub was just across the street, and my father felt that we really should spend a few more moments here before heading back to Budapest. So, we all went to the pub to soak in the atmosphere our ancestors much had felt when they were here.

The pub was tiny, but it seemed that somehow half the village was able to fit inside of it. And, the majority of them were there already when we arrived. We appeared to them as a bunch of strangers, the kind who do not belong or welcomed there. But regardless, we sat down at a table anyway, and my father brought us some drinks before we just sat silently gazing at each other, not sure how to behave next in this increasingly awkward situation. The whole scenario seemed to continue to increase in its awkwardness, and the more and more people peeked at us like we were some kind of alien species come to invade their town. Until the bartender shouted in our direction, asking us where we were from. "Budapest," replied my father. "But my grandfather was from this village. He was born and raised here. We just stopped in to remember him."

"What was his name?" A voice inquired from the back of the pub, from behind a rusty old oak table.

"Meszaros Jozsef!" My father called out, full of pride.

"I don't remember anyone with this name," the bartender began to become very suspicious, so my father continued.

"He built the church right here for the village. I think his name is written on the top of some chair in the temple."

"Meszaros Jozsef." Another stranger added, who was quite close to us before a general murmuring began to ripple throughout the rest of the population in the pub.

"My father knew the chap who founded the building quite well. He was quite a man." Said, one person.

"Isn't he the one who lived two streets away in the big house? I remember him. He was a kind man." Injected another as the chatter from everyone in the tavern began to grow louder. It reminded me almost of an argument that would arise amongst the members of some house of parliament.

"I remember him. The old Joseph. He died many years ago. I saw him a lot in the garden of the church when I was a kid!" Exclaimed someone else.

"He was a friend of our family, too." Chimed in another.

Suddenly, out of nowhere, everyone seemed to remember my great-grandfather, or his daughter, although some of them remembered a boy rather than a girl. But, of course, after this much, who expects people to remember every small detail.

It didn't take five minutes to go from being strangers to becoming the most popular people in the pub. People then began to offer us drinks for all of the good that our family had provided for the village. The weirdest experience, I would have to say, was to see this bunch of strangers coming to us in a similar spirit as people would have welcomed Jesus for showing up in their villages. Everything was covered in a blur of hugs and kisses, and good wishes. The feeling of general happiness and reunion began to take over and control the place in only a matter of minutes.

Someone went to call the priest to open the church gate for us, as we had all the right to return and have a look at what our old man had built. It was truly a glorious moment to be there.

Unfortunately, in the end, we couldn't get in as no one found the minister, and no one else had the keys to the huge gates of the temple.

Nonetheless, we spent a great time in "Perkupa," and we left the pub with big smiles on our faces, having found our ancient home, perhaps even our new one. Just when we were headed back to the car, someone came up to us incredibly happy that they had finally found the vicar who was heading for us right now to open up the Church. People started to gather outside the temple, waiting for the big moment. This was about the time when my father called his mother on his mobile to share the incredible news and thrill that we were experiencing. I didn't hear the conversation going on between my father and grandma, but I soon discovered that I didn't need to. For it was also at that moment, that his face told me everything I needed to know. I suddenly felt that somehow there was something wrong, as I saw the smile slowly disappear from his face only to be replaced very quickly by fear. When he hung up the phone, we were all standing right next to our car, and when he spoke to us, his words came out very matter of fact and clear. "Get in the car. We're going."

Though we were still quite confused, it was one of those moments where we knew that it was best not to ask too many questions, and just do as he said. We hopped in, and my father started the engine right away. Sitting in the back seat, I saw how people started to become a bit confused themselves as we accelerated like bandits fleeing the scene of a crime. It was all a bit surreal seeing the crowd standing in the middle of the square, looking at us, waving at us. I am not sure what was going through their minds. But for me as a kid, at the time, they all looked like some of them were sad, some of them were hopeful that we would return, and most of them were just quite simply drunk.

The silence hung in the car like a smothering awkward wet blanket for many moments as we quietly sat there, not sure how to respond to what had just happened. When finally, my mother broke the silence by asking my father what my grandmother had said on the phone. My father, turning a few shades of red, seemed a bit ashamed of himself. But I still managed to understand as he quietly replied, "I mixed up the town's name, we're not even in the same county."

The Knee

I was about 16 years old, and it was a hot summer day. My school didn't have a schoolyard as it was in the middle of the concrete jungle in the heart of Budapest. So every time our PE teacher wanted to let us play football (or soccer, if you live in the States), we had to walk down to the nearest park, where there was a small concrete court that would better suit our needs. Though I was never really good at football, it was the perfect way to divert my thoughts away from the English exam we were about to write after PE. I always hated the written exams. When I needed to speak in an exam, especially either literature or physics, I shined brightly like a star. But, when I was required to write down the answers, I tended to get very stressed out. To be honest, on that particular day I hadn't really prepared for the exam anyway. I thought the other subjects to be way more important than English, so I prioritised them as such, English is the last possible thing I was thinking of.

As we were playing on the mini football field, someone passed the ball to me, and it came as a bit of a shock to me as I didn't know what to do with it. "What to do? What to do?" I asked myself as a 16-year-old who didn't have a talent for these sort of things. So I tried my best to start imitating what I knew of football stars, moving the ball around like someone who knew what they were doing, trying to trick my opponents. "Fake it til you make it. Right?" But as always, these situations usually end up with someone better coming for the ball and taking it away as if it were nothing and leaving the dummy player standing there with this look on their face, which if you hadn't figured it out by now, that player was me, in this case. You try and put on the best "What? How did he possibly manage to get it away from me? What are the chances?" Kind of faces. This, of course, is very humiliating to watch for anyone who is viewing from the outside.

This time, however, was a bit different, though. I had the ball with me, and though on the inside I was prepared that it would be taken away from me very quickly, I was not expecting the push that came with it. One of my classmates came along and pushed me so hard. I felt like a tree that had been blown over by hurricane-force winds. For the record, I didn't hurt myself at all. After all, I had years of dancing and martial arts behind me, so I remembered how to fall without injuring myself too badly. But I thought it would be appropriate to go with the spirit of the game. I needed to overreact a little bit, kind of like the big stars do in real football. I made that customary hissing noise and waited for the others to get my joke, but apparently my joke caught more attention and concern rather than humour than I had intended.

The PE teacher rushed over to me, with a face that was covered in worry. He asked me if I was doing alright. I almost laughed and was about to tell him, "Of course, I am" when I had a sudden thought about the English exam. The epiphany struck me like a bolt of lightning to my teenage brain. "Hang on a second," I thought to myself. And, I decided to give myself what I thought was an ingenious plan, a try. This, of course, meant milking the situation for all that it was worth and I pretended that I didn't feel too well after all.

"I'm not sure," I replied to the teacher.

"Did you hit your knee?" He asked me. This was when I realised that I was clutching my left knee as the players did on the telly.

"My dad could see him." Offered a boy named, Gregory, one of my classmates who happened to be the son of a surgeon with a pretty high reputation for working at the sports medicine clinic.

At that moment, I knew I had won my case. There will be no exams for me today! All that was left for me to do was go the hospital for a quick check-up, and due to the long queues in Hungarian hospitals, it was very likely that I would not have to return to school at all the rest of the day.

"That would be great. It's better to get this checked out." I said, and let my classmates help me up. I put all of my weight onto Gregory's shoulders and let him help carry me around the field and back to the school.

I was laughing hysterically inside. "What are the odds?" I thought to myself. The sensation of happiness and pride in myself for having gotten away with utterly fooling them got even better and more intense. I thought it through once again about how I would be going away to a different district of the city in this beautiful weather, while the others would still have to suffer through a double English class at school. At this point, it was clear to me that this day could not possibly get any better.

We changed our clothes back in the dressing room, and I tried to do it as slowly as physically possible. After all, why would I rush when I had all day? Also, I was supposed to be injured, and I needed to keep up appearances. I wasn't sure how Greg felt about missing the exam, but I guessed he must have been pretty happy about it too. He probably didn't want to blow his cover, either. I decided to keep playing the invalid for the whole trip through the city, just in case anyone suspected that I was faking. We travelled by underground, and unfortunately, we arrived at the hospital a lot quicker than I would have liked or expected. "Who cares? There are going to be like a dozen or so people ahead of us." I thought. When we stepped into the sports medicine clinic, we went straight for the lift, which did bring us to the level where Greg's father was practicing and then sat on a chair in the aisle. In the meantime, he went to see the receptionist, who I could see from a distance to point at me and then she nodded her head.

I waited no more than two minutes before I was called. People around me, sitting in chairs as I had been, all looked at me. Some of them seemed to be angry, and others were confused. Many of them were looking at my knee, which I still tried to hold with my left hand like I was afraid of losing my patella along the way.

This is where the whole situation began to turn upside down. I suddenly remembered how much we had to wait because of others in line before us when we were at the hospital. In

Hungary, if you are a friend of the doctor, most of the time you are given priority much in the same way you would get an upgrade to first class when you go to the airport; that is if you don't feel like waiting in the queues for a long time. This was the very first time I had experienced how this half of the world lived, now I was the priority, but the problem was I was the only one there with no problems, at least not with my knee, anyway. Thinking back on it now, I am not so sure if the same could be said for my head.

Previously, I considered telling this story to my mother, hoping she would find it funny, but at this point, I felt that she would probably be super angry and disappointed in me.

Greg's father was a very decent man. He probably must have been in his late fifties, at the time, greying hair, blue eyes, and the look of a staunch army officer who knew that time was precious. I am still not sure what Gregory might have said to the nurse to get me in before the others, but it was clear that he handled me as an important patient. We shook hands, he introduced himself, and then he and the nurse lead me into an examination room.

I had to take my trousers off and lay down on the examination table. I was trembling on the inside. So far, this whole thing had just been a good joke, a big waste of time so that I could skip a stupid exam, but suddenly it was all becoming very real to me very quickly. I was laying on an uncomfortable cold table. My parents knew nothing about where I was, I had a doctor standing over me, and other real patients who had very real needs waiting for him to finish with me. "How stupid I must be." The sudden realisation came to my mind.

Though I still didn't want to blow my cover, because so far I had been very stupid, but at least no one had caught on to my shenanigans. Once they figured it out, everyone in the room would know, and what would have been worse? The only thing that could come to mind was all of the ridicule I would receive, as well as anger and disappointment, from everyone once they let everyone at school know that I had faked my injury. So, there was nothing else for me to do but continue to play the part. As soon as the doctor touched my knee, I cried out. I made this hissing sound, not too loud, but just enough to let him know that I felt a bit of pain as a result of falling on the concrete, but it was not that big of a deal. I'll live.

He did a thorough examination and did a bunch of tests on my leg for the next several minutes. I couldn't decide how I should behave, when to hiss or when to shut up. Everything I did was completely random.

After a few minutes, he said that I was fine for now and could wait in the waiting room with the rest of the patients, and he would be back soon. I shuffled out from the little room and resumed my seat next to Greg.

"So, what's up?" He asked me, but I just shrugged.

"I don't know, but I already feel much better." I already had a plan to slowly transition in the following moments to show that my pain was slowly disappearing and I became healthy once again. It was quite hard to play though, sitting in a chair in a room full of angry strangers, who were all staring at me as if I were the devil incarnate.

After a few awkward moments, the doctor came back and called me into his room once again. I now had the chance to regenerate slowly. So, I thought when I stood up, I would hiss a little bit, but by the time I reached the door, I would spectacularly have recovered by at least fifty percent. I don't know why I thought I could play this out. I just felt that I could at the time. So, that is exactly what I did, and somehow, I felt that everyone knew that I was a bit better already.

"Please, have a seat." The man said, and his face showed that he was very serious.

"I am screwed. He knows, he must know. Why else would he be so serious? He is going to tell my parents what I did for sure." The thoughts scrambled around frantically in my head.

The doctor sat down in front of me, and for a few seconds, he was looking at me quietly. At some point, I felt so ashamed that I almost started to cry and apologise before he blew my cover, but then he suddenly started to speak.

"Chris, it's hard to tell you nicely." He began. "Here we go, go ahead," the voice whispered in my head as I held my breath while staring at the floor. "You're going to need surgery on your knee."

For a few seconds, I was just sitting there, and I was sure that I had misunderstood what I just heard. "Say what?" The words flew out of my mouth without even a second thought.

"I know it's not a nice thing to hear, an operation might sound scary, but it seems to me that the pain you feel is caused by damage to your cartilage, which requires surgery. First, we will need to do an X-ray, and you might want to call your parents so you can arrange an appointment with the hospital. I am happy to do the surgery, as it is a straight forward process."

His voice trailed off as I stopped listening to what he was saying. I saw black dots appear in the periphery of my sight, and I was sure that I would have fainted if I hadn't sat down. I don't remember exactly how long I sat there, but I remember when we finally left the room, the last words were about my parents getting in touch as soon as possible; so we could arrange the surgery. Greg was looking at me, surprised. "What happened?"

"I'm not sure." I must have looked pretty bad as he immediately helped me to sit down. "I'll need surgery."

I don't remember the exact details of how we got back to school. It was all a bit of a blur. All I remember is promising myself that I would never fake any other pain or injury in my life, and I hoped to God that my parents would never hear about this day.

We missed the first half of the English lesson, but as it usually happens to me, this did not obstruct the teacher from making us write the test as the second part of the double English class.

As awful as that day was, I was in constant fear for weeks

that this whole thing would somehow reach my parents, so I stayed low on the radar and tried not to bring too much attention to myself. I remember a few days later, Greg asked me if I had a chance to talk to my parents, as his dad had not heard back from them yet. I told him that I didn't think I would need to have the surgery after all. Then, let it go. I hoped that it would never pop up again. Luckily enough for me, it never has, until now, of course.

The Cat Litter

Usually, when you don't own a home, you are forced to rent out a flat. Now, this may be easy if you are on your own, a bit more complex when it's two of you. But when you add in the equation of two cats into the mix, this makes searching for one a bit more difficult. Seeing as how the majority of landlords prefer to have tenants without pets, which I understand if we're talking about people with large dogs as they might feel a bit more uncomfortable in a small apartment. Not to mention, they might bark all day or all night long, which could keep you from having a healthy relationship with your neighbours. But cats are a completely different story altogether. As long as you are willing to pay the extra deposit to ensure the landlord that no damages will be done on the part of the cat, or that you are willing to clean up or fix said damages yourself, there is no logical reason why they shouldn't allow you to have them in your flat. Cats are usually small creatures, so they do fine in a flat, most of the time.

For anyone who owns cats, I'm sure you understand that they are pretty easy pets to have, considering they usually keep to themselves and mine in particular likes to sleep for at least 18 hours a day. Can you imagine that? 18 hours a day. If only it were socially acceptable for humans to be allowed to sleep that much. I figured this out, as we always have a camera system installed in our flat for security purposes, so I had the chance to check their daily routine on many occasions via the security video footage.

These two little funny creatures sleep almost two and a half times more than the average person spends their time at work. And when they're finally awake, they barely do anything that requires too much effort. Yes, they may play for two to three minutes at a time here and there, but they mostly eat, drink, poo, and watch birds for hours at a time out the window. These truly are probably the luckiest and happiest creatures on earth, getting everything they ask for immediately without any obligations to return the favour whatsoever. There is, however, only one really important responsibility you cannot forget when it comes to living with these furry little balls of fun. And, that of course, is cleaning out the litter box at least once or twice a day. That is something which you only get to understand when the four-legged duke of the flat decides to leave his mark in the litter after an abundant dinner. For a few moments, it may be possible to leave it like that. The cloud coming forth from the litter box fades away after a while, but when you procrastinate to clean it out throughout the day; then, it is no exaggeration to say that by the time you finally get to it, it's pretty much game over for you. And, this is something I had to learn on my own.

It was a long and busy work-week when I unintentionally forgot to clean out their litter box during the evening. The next day I went to work, only to come home late at night. As soon as I entered the flat, I felt like someone who just got a sip of a rotten egg soup which had probably been sitting out for about a year. Except, this was worse, it was as if all of the liquid from the soup had evaporated and I instead tasted it through my nose. At that moment, I knew I was never going to let that happen again. I did the only thing which came to mind as a temporary solution. I took the air freshener from the top cupboard, covered my face with the sleeve of my hoodie, and started to spray the air. After this, I needed to sit down for a bit, as I had started to run out of oxygen, but I was ready to face the litter box once I got some of my energy back. I sat there for about ten seconds when I felt that I couldn't catch my breath. I stood up and headed to the living room window, but I suddenly felt dizzy and weak. The god-awful smell still hung in the air, so I thought the air freshener wasn't doing its job. This caused me to continue to spray the air all around me as I was moving along, hoping that I would finally be able to catch some relief. It didn't happen. I was in very bad shape within only a matter of seconds. I didn't quite understand what was happening to me, but my thoughts by then had become unclear and foggy. All I knew was that I wanted to reach the window as quickly as possible, but the closer I came the further away it seemed, and my legs didn't have the power to take me there.

    After what felt like an eternity, I finally got there. I flung the window open as a drunk man would open his door when he gets home. I tried to get a secure grasp on the handle, but it was like trying to solve a complex puzzle single-handedly.

    When the fresh oxygen finally reached my lungs, I felt like someone who was being reborn. The energy came flowing back to my limbs, and my thoughts began to clear.

It was about this time that I began to notice the lack of smell of roses, which is what I had come to expect from the air freshener which I had so diligently sprayed in the last few minutes. As my vision slowly started to clear up, I took a look at the bottle, but what I saw made me think that I was probably still not seeing too clearly. Or, at least, I hoped not. Then suddenly the puzzle pieces began to match up. This was not air freshener at all. It was shoe impregnation spray, the kind that you closely apply to your shoes to make them water-resistant, and strongly recommended to apply it outdoor.

I can honestly say this made it into the top 5 of dumbest moments in my life. So, I just sat there next to the window for several minutes, trying to clear out my lungs. It was at this point that I realised my cats had gone to the furthest possible point of the flat, next to the storage room, a place where the air constantly flew into the flat from under the door gap. The look they gave me was very easy to read, no subtitles necessary. Their eyes were broadcasting a single and very loud message, "Humans, the bottom of the evolutionary chain."

The Award

People probably think that getting an award is the best thing ever. They never think about the stress it comes with. You have to dress up nice, make sure you look good, in case you have to make a speech. You can't eat or drink a lot during the ceremony, as you basically have to look perfect for the cameras and other people who voted for you, because they think you are doing something right. So, that's the last night you want to prove the opposite. I had the wonderful chance of getting an award at an event where lots of celebrities were present, including the number one media person in Hungary. He was very famous, as well as was much older than me, and way more respected.

The event started in the morning, and I showed up at the very beginning, as I was very excited about meeting all of these people. Famous people joined the event as presenters from the US and the UK, too. The whole thing felt very prestigious. Cameras were shooting everything, even at the lunch areas.

All the food and drinks were free, and people got the chance to meet each other, talk and of course, take photos together in front of the press. I got lost in the hundreds of people, as I wasn't that famous. Telenovela viewers may have known my voice pretty well, theatre-loving people would know my face, but these people were moving on a completely different level. They were all proper famous, and rich.

This is why it was so very unpleasant when I queued up for the toilet. Just for the record, I have never seen a queue in front of a men's toilet. It might be a usual sight to find in front of the women's toilet, as I know there is usually always a bunch of ladies waiting there to freshen up and check their mascara. But since the invention of the urinal, it is rare to find a queue in front of the gentlemen's loo, even if it is a big event. Or at least that is what I have noticed. I suppose this is just a testament to the fact that I don't go to very many of these types of functions. But, oh well.

It just so happened that in this particular theatre, where this event was being held, there were only three urinals. So if you had any business to do, you needed to do it quickly to make room for the next guy. As I was standing in line, I was looking at the people around me, and I was fascinated by how much money it appeared that they had spent on the event. For me, it seemed like a huge and unnecessary waste of money, even though I was politely invited to attend this event, to be presented an award. But what do I know? Thinking back on it now that kind of mindset makes me sound kind of stuck up, or ignorant. Not really sure which.

At the time, all I knew was that I needed to concentrate on the task at hand, to get to the toilet and do my business as quickly as humanly possible. Suddenly, I realised that the person standing behind me in the queue was the number one TV presenters in the country. "Wow!" I thought, even though I was a guest, I felt like a fan who walked in from the streets, and I had to suppress the urge to ask for an autograph. Back in the days before selfies were a thing, we pretty much were all about the autograph. But I didn't have a pen or any paper with me, so I somehow was able to contain myself, unlike usual as you have come to know me throughout my stories, and I decided not to ask him for his autograph — score one to me for using my better judgment, and acting like a polite human being.

The queue went very slowly, and at one point the bells began to ring, meaning that the ceremony was now about to continue in the big room.

"Come on." I thought. I wasn't sure when my award section was going to take place, all I knew was that I was tired and anxious.

I tried out some very interesting food at the open dining area a few minutes before, but I purposely avoided eating too much not to be part of another funny story.

It took a few additional minutes, but I finally made it. I was finally at the urinal, and I could have my sacred relief. I went for the middle one, so there were two other people close to me, and a bunch of others behind us in the queue. I didn't think it was going to turn out unpleasant, but I managed to relax my muscles so much that at the end of my relief I had like the loudest fart ever made in human history. It was so loud that I even heard it echoing from the wall causing a surround sound effect.

"Did they notice it was me?" was my first thought. People laughed, and as I looked right, the man standing next to me looked at me with this face like "Now that was something mate." Then I realised, the TV presenter might still be standing behind me. So, I finished my business and slowly turned around.

He was standing right in front of me, his arms were crossed over his chest, and he looked at me with his eyes wide open, his eyebrows up. It was as if his face were asking me, "Are you serious?" It was utterly humiliating. I went to wash my hands, and I suddenly felt like I was back in school, where I was bullied all the time. I was rushing back to the big hall to sit down in my seat and hoped that no one would recognise me in a few minutes as they forgot about the incident.

Soon the lights went down, and the afore-mentioned TV presenter appeared on the stage while the music started. I went lower in my chair, hoping he wouldn't look at me. After a few minutes, he suddenly made it clear that he was now going to present the category's winner, which I came for in the first place.

"No. No. No." I was begging in my head not to be called. When I finally heard my name, everyone was clapping, and I needed to go up to the stage. It felt like I had won an all-expenses-paid trip to hell. My pulse was rushing, and my face was red. I went to the stage, and then I approached the guy, to shake his hand. The moment he looked at me, his jaw dropped, and his mouth gaped open. Yet, he had the biggest smile I had ever seen, and I had one of the most humiliating moments on stage — hopefully, my first and last time to experience something like this. But knowing me, this will most certainly not be the case.

Luckily for me, it wasn't necessary for me to give a speech. I was grateful for this, amid my humiliating and mortifying misery, there was no amount of picturing the audience naked or in their underwear that could have eased my uncomfortable predicament. The more I thought about it, the more anxious I became, and I decided wisely that the best course of action was to get off the stage and run home as quickly as possible. Hoping that something more humiliating would occur to someone else and cause everyone to forget about little 'ole me and my not so little fart.

The Graduation Ceremony

Going back to school as an adult is always a big decision for anyone. Because of a serious spine disorder that I was born with, which only manifested itself after I started work as a graduate artist, life gave me a choice to change my profession and I had to go back to school once again. I needed a career path that was going to be less physically challenging. Since I have been programming as a hobby, from the time I was a kid, I knew that the best field of study for me to pursue was that of software engineering. What I enjoy most about coding is that it gives me the chance to use my creative strengths, as well as my logic, to craft something seemingly from nothing. It is an activity that relaxes me while challenging me and improving the daily function of my mind. The more I learned about IT, I realised just how many things I didn't know just yet. It excited me the same way the secrets of our very own galaxy and universe excite explorers. But I digress.

The day you finally receive your diploma, that exciting little piece of paper that proves to the rest of the world just how much time you spent honing your craft, and emptying your wallet, is a pretty big day. During this experience, I had accrued good grades, good friends, and most importantly, a good reputation. Some of our professors already knew of me as an artist, and I always got the feeling that they somehow respected me for leaping to start my life over, by studying as well as sometimes working for 12 hours a day.

It was a very hot June day, in Budapest. I did not invite anyone to the ceremony, except for my wife Laura, because she insisted on coming. She, of all people, knows how preoccupied I can be. So, she gathered my suit and put it into a protective bag at home before she headed to the university. We arranged to meet there at 15:00, so we could have at least another hour before the ceremony started. That is exactly how it happened, we met and had a great walk just outside the building, all the while carrying on a conversation of which I cannot precisely remember the contents. But at some point, she noticed that I was still in my shorts and sneakers, and she sent me to change my clothes because in thirty minutes I would need to look smart.

I could see how crowded the large hall already was with relatives and friends of everyone else who was about to get their diploma. I passed by the hall and went straight to the loo to change. I had my bag of clothes with me, so I went right into a cabin, and started to dress up — first, the shirts, of course, and then the tie. "I'll need a mirror for that," I thought to myself. So, I hung it around my neck loosely and set about taking out the suit itself. It was in perfect condition. The standard by which I measured this was that no one, even I from the looks of it, could tell by my suit that we were living with cats.

I felt genuinely grateful to Laura for cleaning it and bringing it to me. I knew how important it was to her for me to look my best.

I began to run through the checklist in my head out loud, naming off each thing one by one to make sure that I had everything I needed before departing the cabin. "Here are the shoes," they were as shiny and clean as a new pair. But I had the overwhelming feeling that one usually gets right after leaving the house, that I forgot something. "What am I missing?" I asked my subconscious once I realised there was nothing left in the bag. Yet, I still felt like there was something else I needed. Then, it finally dawned on me. "The trousers."

I was standing in the cabin in my khaki shorts and became very confused very quickly. I double-checked, hoping that I had just not seen them at first, but I quickly realised to my horror that there were truly no trousers to be found hiding in the suit protector bag.

"That's odd," I thought out loud and decided to move out of the cabin to see about the situation with Laura. On my way out, I checked myself in the mirror, made a Windsor knot on my tie, and proudly left the toilet. On the upside, I did look perfectly smart on my shirt, tie, and suit. The only downside, however, was the fact I was still wearing these garish khaki shorts. The type you usually only wear to a BBQ which you host in the comfort and privacy of your garden. They, of course, left my knees and the rest of my legs completely exposed, and as your eyes panned further down, you could see my white socks; which I hoped would be covered by my missing pair of trousers. And, for the finishing touch, a classic pair of Oxford shoes.

Now it is quite true that I usually couldn't care less about what I am wearing, and though my wife always tries to do something about it, I generally hate clothing as it is completely out of my span of interests as is what I generally look like. This is such an apparent quality of mine, that when we went shopping in Hungary, I would normally sit in the shopping centre outside of the store and Laura would have to convince the shop assistants to allow her to bring out some of the clothes to check the sizes on me. In many of these stores, they knew us both so well, and they would just let her do it. This is how much I am not willing to cooperate when it comes to clothing, and even in this mindset, at that particular moment, even I felt that being in that set of clothes on that day, finally receiving my second diploma was all a bit too odd.

So, I approached my wife with a bit of caution, asking her if she knew anything about the location of my missing trousers. She was rather terrified when she looked at me and instantly gave me the impression that my missing trouser was nowhere nearby.

"I told you to pack them before I left, don't you remember?" She asked.

I didn't.

"So, what do we do now?" I asked, trying to act like this was somehow a completely normal situation to find oneself in. All the while, other people's family members began to stare at me, as well as professors; with raised eyebrows.

"I don't know," was all she could say. It was certainly one of those situations in our lives where I could tell Laura indeed had no idea how we were going to proceed from here.

"Hi Chris, I like your clothes." A friend of mine just appeared out of nowhere with his family, everyone looking super smart, of course. "I hope you come in those shorts." He joked, and all of them laughed.

"I think I will," I responded and then watched them go into the hall. All the while, I remember thinking to myself that it would not be the end of the world if I had to.

Looking at my wife, it was clear she thought otherwise. She grabbed me by the wrist, like someone would a child, and pulled me out of the university.

"We're going to look for new trousers." She said, and it was quickly apparent that she was not joking. We had less than 20 minutes before the ceremony would start, and we had seven minutes until we found a second-hand clothing shop on the first floor of a bus station complex. It just so happened that it was above a Chinese fast-food restaurant. Considering how I was currently, at least halfway, dressed in my dapper attire, you can imagine how I received quite a few awkward looks from people as I walked into this thrift store. This is usually the place where you find people who have to shop in the budget section, and just then, I didn't look like someone who should be shopping in the budget section.

My wife searched frantically through the trousers, it took her a few minutes to go through each potential candidate she came across, but none of them seemed to be a good fit.

Finally, we asked the shop assistant if she could help us and she pointed us to the end of the room; where there was a huge basket of clothing, things which people donated to the shop. They gave each item away for 100 HUF, which was worth something like £0.25 back then.

At the top of the stack, there was a pair of dark green trousers. They were very worn, very ugly, and smelled like death. Laura pointed at them and announced, "We're out of time. You're going to wear this."

She didn't even bother to look any further, she just took the trousers, and we immediately queued up to the till. The cashier looked at us like she had never seen humans before. It has had something to do with my weird half-smart outfit. I guess she was trying to fit the puzzle pieces of my odd appearance together in her head. We did not have time to stand there and wonder about what was going through her head at the time, as my wife had said before, we were out of time. So, we quickly ran back to the university, and me to the toilet as quickly as possible in a last-ditch effort to make it to the ceremony on time.

When I changed, I realised that this was probably not the best choice of trousers that we could have gone with. However, they were the only choice available in the time constraints that we were under. Once I got out of the toilet, my wife began to laugh so hard that her knees buckled and she fell onto them on the floor. She was completely hysterical. At one point, she was laughing so hard that she was crying. Occasionally, she would open her eyes and look at me again only to lose it all over again.

The trousers were so big on me that even a belt made no difference. It was quite clear that they were made for a man who was at least two feet taller, and one stone heavier. The belt area was so wide that Laura could have stood up in the trousers with me, and it would have been perfectly comfortable. Even though I folded the bottom parts of the leg area twice, they were still way too long. So, I literally looked like an ugly, smelly clown, who was now as ready as he ever would be to get his diploma.

After Laura was finally able to stop laughing and speak again, she began trying to convince me not to go into the hall room dressed that way. She said it would be better for me if I did not turn up at all. They might give me the diploma after the ceremony. But I was not convincible. I had worked my ass off for this piece of paper, and I was going to be damned sure that I was going to be there when they told everyone I was the class leader of the year.

This, of course, turned out to be one of the most interesting decisions of my life. The great hall was packed with thousands of people. The room was gradually higher and higher as you walked to the back, full of school desks. There are steps at both sides of the room allowing people to go back, and the main area, where the professors usually presented, was at the very front; at the lowest point of the hall. The students were all sitting in rows in the hall, so for several minutes, no one noticed what I was wearing. Until, of course, I was called out to shake hands with the professors and take my diploma.

I would have to say that walk was probably the longest walk of my life. People started applauding when my name was announced as the class leader. So, I got out of the school desk and started to go down to the front. I almost fell at least three times, maybe more, as the trousers just went down and down, again and again. The folded sections, which were right above my shoes, decided to unfold themselves as I got lower. Meaning, by the time I got down, I needed one hand to even keep the trousers on me. But this did not solve the issue that I could barely move.

I clearly remember how every one of my professors looked dead at the trousers I was wearing with the clear and obvious expression that they could not believe what they were witnessing.

After I finally got my degree, I faced the truth that not only would I need to go back to the top where I came from, but this time I also had to carry my diploma with me. As I began my trek back, I started sweating. I smelled from the shitty pants, and I needed to shift all of my focus into ensuring that I would not fall over.

I realise now why people say that graduation is usually something for you and your loved ones to cherish and never forget. I most certainly believe that in our case, this memory is guaranteed to last for all eternity.

Violent Brittany

Out of all of the workplaces in my life, I would have to say that this one was definitely one of the strangest. Businesswise, it was right in the middle of the buzz. They tried to hire people with the best professional qualities they could find, and they needed every job to be completed as quickly as possible. Due to the fact this company was quite successful, money was not an issue for them. The point was to get the right people who could work quickly and efficiently. This might be all well and good as far as intentions go, and in a way it was, and for the most part, seemed to be working out pretty well for them. But in the meantime, it resulted in a workplace that was full of people who all wanted to get higher and higher up the corporate ladder, not caring about anything else but their jobs or the people they had to crawl over to get to the top. So, as you can imagine, conversations were shallow and artificial, with no real connections made between people, because everyone saw each other as competition. Having been a part of a workplace later that was completely opposite of everything that I just described to you, shows me how sad I truly must have been there, and how isolated I must have felt. Being the kind of person I am, I was desperate to make connections. I just had to find the proper way to do that.

Sitting on the sofa in the reception area was a big part of my daily life during lunch break. Whenever it was raining, and I was unable to go out for a walk in the park, I would just sit on the sofa reading a book, or just watching other people silently. I must have looked like some kind of sociopath. If someone came along, I smiled, and if someone started a conversation with me, I was always more than happy about it. But this never lasted more than a moment or so before they moved on to the next thing, everyone and everything felt very busy here. One day though, as I was sitting there, I noticed a few people standing around the news board where the company representatives would post the latest corporate news. They were all talking loudly, and for the first time at this company, I heard laughter as well. "So they must be humans after all." I thought.

One of the guys in glasses said, "Look, Matt is now a senior. It's now official then, so he must have to give-up the prince title." This was followed by everyone bursting into laughter once again. What they were talking about didn't make any sense to me, but it must have been pretty hilarious as they were all laughing so hard.

In a second, my boss appeared out of nowhere and hailed me. "You alright?" He asked.

"Yeah, sure. How about you?" I replied.

"Not too bad, thank you. What are you up to?" He saw me with my smartphone in my hand.

"I'm looking for a new voice recorder online," I responded. "My old one is dead."

"Oh gosh, I have a voice recorder, which I got as a Christmas present, and I never use it." He seemed quite excited about the subject for a second.

"Wow, and are you planning to use it?" I asked.

"No, I have no idea what I would use it for. I don't think I'll ever need it." He answered.

I genuinely hadn't talked that much with my boss before about something which was not related to work. For a second, I felt like I had finally broken the ice.

"Ah, I see, would you consider selling it, then?" I inquired.

"No," he shook his head, then turned around and left. It was surreal. It felt so unreal that I remember beginning to laugh out of nowhere. This was most likely the time something changed in me, and I felt I didn't really care about anything anymore. I was simply going to get myself into a conversation on my own. What could I lose?

I went to the board, where there was only one guy standing now, and he was approximately the same age as I. I started to scan the corporate updates with my eyes. Out of the corner of my eye, I caught that he had looked at me for a second, so I raised my eyebrows and nodded like we knew each other. "Say something. Be friendly." I thought and said the only thing that came to my mind. "So, Matt is a senior now, huh?" I had no idea who Matt was. "It's now clear then. He is no longer a prince."

The guy started laughing. "I know. That's crazy."

Suddenly, I felt incredibly proud. Even though I just repeated back what I had heard before, and had absolutely no idea what I was talking about. I still felt like I finally found the key to making friends here. The holy grail, and now I had to use it.

"See you," said my newest friend before he departed. I was over the top on the inside. I still had some time from my lunch break, so I thought I would read through the announcements, and get myself more familiar with the others. A bit later, a lady appeared. She seemed like she was looking for something on the board but couldn't find it.

"That's crazy," I said out of the blue, shaking my head, eager to be involved in a new conversation.

"What?" She asked, with a kind smile.

"Matt is now a senior. I guess he is no longer a prince." I answered.

"What do you mean?" She responded.

I froze for a second. I had no idea how to reply. "Well, you know Matt." I stuttered.

"I'm afraid I don't, is he from accounting?" She asked.

My eyes were wide open now. I felt like someone who had just jammed a fork into an electric socket in the wall. For a second, I hesitated, and then I did the only reasonable thing I could do. I pretended that I had suddenly found something on the board that was interesting enough to divert my attention. At the bottom of the board, there was a piece of paper, which said that we had a new Data Security Officer. The name of the person was not printed, but written with a pen like they didn't know the name at the time the announcement was printed. The handwriting was awfully ugly, and I could barely read it. But it looked like it said, "Violent Brittany."

I felt this was my chance to divert the lady's attention as well and make her laugh, thus, securing her as a friend for life. Because as we all learn in kindergarten, that is how relationships are supposed to work out, right?

"Ah, look at this," I said. "The new Data Security Officer is called Violent Brittany." I smiled at her like someone complicit in a crime. "Interesting choice, isn't it? To put a violent person in charge."

She looked at me quite suspiciously and then checked the piece of paper. "Yeah, that is Violet Brittany, not violent." She corrected me, and she did not begin to laugh as I had anticipated. But, no matter, I believed I could still do something about it so that I didn't leave it like that.

"Well, it could be." I continued. "But we can't really be certain, as it is so ugly written that you can hardly read it. I would bet on Violent Brittany."

The woman's face became quite serious just then, and she looked directly at me. "That's true, it's quite ugly, but I wrote it in a rush at the last minute. And, it is Violet for sure, as that is me. I am Violet Brittany."

At first, being full of myself, I thought she was kidding. I was still smiling and was about to laugh. My eyebrows threatened to disappear into my hairline as they travelled so high on my forehead as I looked at her and waited for her to reveal she was joking. It took me a few seconds to realise, however, that I would surely die in this place with no friends.

That's Life

The French Wind

Ah, Paris! The land of romance, lights, and great food. Once upon a time. The best place to go if you were planning on having the most romantic days of your life. But in all seriousness, Paris is always an amazing place to travel to, especially, when it is a trip that includes plans to spend most of the time at one of the world's greatest theme parks. However, all of this fun can be very exhausting.

It was certainly the perfect place to lose yourself in its magic. Laura and I spent the majority of our time walking through the park, drinking in the orange glow of the setting sun, and how it painted all of the clouds in different hues of pink and purple as they lay lazily across the evening sky; making all of the grass and trees of the park glitter like something you would imagine in an enchanted forest with a vast peaceful meadow that had suddenly come to life out of a fairy tale storybook right before our very eyes. The dancing light on her beautiful skin and in her starry eyes that looked on me so lovingly. I felt that we had truly stepped into the pages of some kind of romance novel, where I was the hero, and she was the beautiful woman that I found myself very lucky to be with. It seemed like we walked and talked for hours because we probably did. You can't visit Paris without being swept up in its spell that obviously comes with the proviso to turn everyone there into gooney twitter-pated fools.

When we got back to the apartment, which we had rented on the edge of Paris just before midnight, it took a lot of effort to get to the fourth floor of this concrete building, and it was the highest level of the building. There were outdoor stairs that lead us up, but there was no lighting to speak of, only the light of the moon which only slightly lit each step. So visibility was almost nil. At the careful pace we were travelling, it took about five minutes to reach the top, and by then we didn't have any steam left in our bodies, as we had pretty much just walked across the entire city that day.

So as not to ruin the romantic mood of this entire evening experience, I had been holding in a huge fart for several minutes. Because of this, I let Laura go on before me on the steps. As I said, I was very tired, so I told her that I would come in a minute after taking a short break. I took a look behind me to make sure the coast was clear. It was just me and no one else, but who can tell; it was super dark. I continued my way up the stairs, and slowly let out what I felt was probably the longest fart in the world. Or, at least, that I have ever experienced in my entire life. It must have lasted for at least eight seconds, yet it made no sound. It was the silent but deadly sort of farts, the kind that tends to either linger or follow you if you stand in their cloud of methane for too long. It was so powerful and smelly that just being in its presence made me feel dizzy and lightheaded only after a few seconds. So for the sake of Laura's survival, as well as my own, I knew that I needed to stop. Suddenly, a voice came out of the dark. And, I guess because

I was so disoriented from breathing in all of those fumes, I wasn't sure if that sound came from my mouth or my asshole.

    I slowly turned back on the stairs, and out of nowhere saw a guy, who must not have been any older than 22 years old. The sound was coming from him, and he was obviously choking on the noxious fumes that had come from my ass, not the deep guttural voice that I thought had. He used both of his hands to fan the air violently around his face, and from what I could see through the dense darkness, he looked furiously at me. The only thing I could think was, "whoops!" As he was not there only seconds ago. I quickly ran upstairs, to escape into the apartment and hope that Laura would never notice what happened.

    The next morning we woke up a bit late as we were really tired from our trip around the city yesterday. There was a lot of noise in the parking area out in front of the apartment complex. As we passed the cars, the noise became louder and louder. Finally, I walked to the right and saw this group of young people, sitting on top of cars, laughing very hard. When one of them noticed me looking at them, I realised I recognised the guy who had been standing in the stairway behind me the previous night. He obviously remembered me too, because he pointed right at me in front of everyone. Then, he started to shout something in French over and over again. The rest of the group proceeded to burst into laughter, even louder than the last time. They were laughing so obnoxiously that one guy nearly fell from the bonnet of the car.

Laura looked at me, very confused. "Why are they looking at us?" She asked. "What are they laughing at?"

"I have no idea," I responded as inconspicuous as possible. But I was very sure that we left the car park even more quickly than I was inconspicuous.

What she doesn't know about last night won't hurt me. Right?

The Explanation

I hate chaos. Whenever there is a way to create order out of a mess, that gives me this inexplicable calming feeling, something like a profound satisfaction, this is why I do my best to live by the rules, which with few exceptions, I find pretty reasonable. And, that's why I don't usually skip queues if it's not a life or death situation. For the most part, I find them fair and reasonable, even if I have had to wait in one for a long time without being able to sit down. Who am I kidding? I am about as impatient as everyone else and waiting in a queue for a while sucks.

One day though, something really interesting happened. My wife, Laura, and I were standing in a queue at the shop, waiting to be called to one of the tills. My thoughts were all about my journey back to Budapest the following day. I, for one, hate flying. Can't stand it. The reason for this is because I always get the feeling before departure that my plane will somehow be in the 0.000001% (or less) that is destined to crash. And, always I know deep down that it is probably rubbish, but this does not stop my brain from thinking about it. So, inevitably, when I am stressing out, some social anxiety kicks in that causes me to act so weird that retrospectively, I always feel ashamed of myself later. But for some reason, as these awkward situations are occurring, the actions feel completely natural to me.

So, we are there in a shop in Brighton, in the middle of the queue. We have two vegan meal deals in our hands, and the only thing I can think of is that I'm going to die tomorrow when the plane crashes. And, the only thing I will be able to think about while the plane is going down is how cheap I was that I wanted to spend my last evening with my wife at the beach with only two simple sandwiches. "What was wrong with me?" I scolded myself. "I should take her to a restaurant instead, so when the jet is falling out of the sky, I can at least be happy inside that I didn't try to save money on our last supper together." Said another voice in my head.

This whole chain of thoughts went through my head within a matter of seconds, and by the time we were finally called by the cashier to step forward and pay, I already knew that I no longer wanted to buy these sandwiches. I looked at Laura and declared, "Let's go to a restaurant."

"Okay," she said, after a brief second of confusion, and she turned around to take her sandwich back to the shelf we had taken it from.

Now here's the thing, when it comes to my social anxiety and when it fully kicks in, I am terrible at ending things. Closing conversations, halting activities, saying goodbyes, etc. If someone were to watch me as I go through this turmoil, as a spectator from the outside looking in, attempting to do any of these things in public, they would probably think that I had some sort of mental disorder. This, however, may very well explain why I felt the terrible need to go to the cashier, who had already waved at me, and I explain my situation. He gave me the sign, and I felt that this came with a responsibility to meet his expectations, and I, as a kind

Brightonian, didn't want to let him down. So, I stepped ahead and walked to the guy who was standing behind the till.

"Look," I began. "I am not going to buy the sandwiches after all. We are going to put them back where we found them."

He looked at me and nodded. I couldn't tell exactly, but I thought I saw something odd crossing his face. I turned around, began to walk towards my wife, and the feeling that the cashier might have felt sorry for me just seemed to get stronger and stronger. But, why would he feel sorry for me? I have no reason for him to feel sorry for me. Except if maybe--Oh god! Then it dawned on me. He thinks that I can't pay for it. Just then, the world turned upside down. I had come a long way in life, and no one could be prouder of the fact that I could pay for my food, than I. Now, here is this guy, thinking the worst of me, and feeling sorry for me. This didn't feel right at all. "I'm going to explain to him," I told Laura and turned around again. And, though I heard her saying a loud and worried, "What?" I had already made up my mind and started to walk back towards the counter.

By the time I got back to the till an elderly lady was already paying for her things. They both looked at me, confused, but I didn't care. I needed to say what I had been rehearsing during my walk back to the till. "Hi there, sorry for interrupting. Look, I know you probably think I am too poor to pay for these sandwiches, but here's the thing; there is nothing like that going on."

I caught the old lady looking at the cashier, confused, and the guy looking back at Laura with hesitation on his face. He was clearly unsure of how to react to my sudden reappearance and inexplicable need to exposit on the situation.

"As a matter of fact," I continued. "I could pay for even more sandwiches if I wanted, that's not a problem. But the thing is, I decided to take my wife to a restaurant. So, now you know the whole story."

For a second, I thought I would get a response. But all the guy did was open his mouth, take a breath, and then stood there frozen, just staring. I slowly looked around, and clearly, everyone else in the shop noted what I said. This was good enough for me, so I felt I had gotten what I wanted, however unnecessary my actions were. So, I nodded proudly with a smile on my face, more to myself than anyone else around me, and turned back once again for the last time.

I still recall the shocked look Laura gave me before turning around. However, at the time, I did not care. All I knew was that we were going to have the best last supper ever before my impending death the next day.

The Army General

When it comes to putting things on your CV, it comes with a level of responsibility. Even if the facts are fundamentally correct or valid, you need to be sure to double-check your CV from time to time, to make sure that you do not leave anything on there that you are not completely certain about. When I put "Basic German Speaking" on my CV, into the relevant section, it felt just right. I have an Austrian/German heritage, I also lived in Germany for a short period of time, and I am quite comfortable speaking about many basic things to the point of telling others what kind of cats I have, which is pretty much the end of the conversations I'm having in German anyway, as most people lose interest in me by this point. I never thought that mentioning "Basic German" on my CV would ever lead me into any trouble, but clearly, I was wrong.

The thing with CV's is that they never show you what a person is capable of, but they rather show you what a person thinks of themselves and what would be good to mention to others in order to make themselves look appealing. Much like how a person is usually on their best behaviour on a first date, you want to put the best possible perception of yourself forward in order to receive the best possible outcome of the situation, except with a CV. This data is then filtered by another person, the interviewer or the HR representative who has a completely different prism through which to view these qualities and qualifications, and it is tailored to the specifications of the desired function of the role and if they think you would be best for it. By the time your CV is processed, someone will have a series of impressions about you, and you won't necessarily fulfil all of these impressions exactly on the day of the interview, fortunately, and sometimes, unfortunately. This is most likely why mentioning my heritage to my former colleagues gave them the impression that I am perfect in German, even though I have never said such a thing. And as we all know, when you assume, it is very easy to turn yourself into the first three letters of that word.

One day the phone rang on my desk, which I immediately found odd as I was not even aware that the device was there before then. I worked for the company as an engineer for several months, but it never came to my attention that there was a landline in front of me. First, I looked around to see if anyone else noticed it too, but no one else seemed to be paying attention to the ringing sound. So, I slowly reached out my arm to the phone, but suddenly I heard a low voice behind me. "Chris, sorry about that, we need your help." It was the CEO himself, along with some other people from the management. He looked like someone who had just been running, his face coloured with stress, and his voice a little higher pitched than usual.

"At the end of the phone, it is a Bayern General, and he has a question, but--" He paused for a moment to look at his colleagues, with a bit of shame in his expression. "We don't really understand what he is saying. His English is not the best, so we thought maybe you could talk to him in German."

While he told me all of that, other colleagues of mine had gathered around as well full of curiosity, starting to form a bit of a semicircle around me. I had nothing in my mind to give as any response, and I suppose you could say that my brain was temporarily down as it tried to process what was happening to me at that moment. Therefore, I waited a few seconds, took a deep breath, and reached to the receiver without any further hesitation.

"Guten Tag, meine name ist Chris, wie kann ich helfen?" The words flowed from my mouth without much effort or hesitation, as I greeted the caller, introduced myself, and asked how I could be of help.

My pride did a little happy dance in my soul, and I could have sworn that I heard a choir of cherubs singing above me, as an imaginary halo appeared around my head. I felt in that moment that I had been completely transformed into something that my great-grandfather would have been proud of. The response from the other side of the receiver came immediately, and I was just able to catch the greetings before the sudden darkness took place in my mind.

There are those situations in life where you want to listen very much, but you simply can't seem to follow what the other person is saying. This was maths for me. Throughout high school, I had to learn everything on my own to get good grades, as my teacher's words were usually lost on me most of the time, and I was left to do nothing but stare at the blackboard with that profound, "I must be so dumb" feeling which sucks any courage I may possess right out of my mind and body. This same feeling from my youth suddenly found me at that moment and completely consumed my entire body, as I was listening to the German-speaking person on the other side of the world.

It is worth mentioning that if you are a native Hungarian, there is no way on Earth that you don't understand another Hungarian, even if they are living on the other side of the country. This is because it is such a small place on the map. The same is not true, however, for German. Go to the north, east, or maybe the south parts of Germany, and you will find that each will sound completely different. Not to mention, the different ways to pronounce these same words in other countries like Austria or Switzerland.

For me listening to this man on the other side of the phone, was almost like listening to Freddie Mercury singing "Another One Bites the Dust" at school in Budapest when I was six. Not saying that listening to this man was anywhere near as awesome or enjoyable of an experience, I am saying that I could not for the life of me understand a single word he said, but I had to appear like someone who could, to look cool in front of everyone else. Except, instead of schoolmates, it was my colleagues now who were looking up to me.

I just nodded from time to time with the receiver in my hand, as if the General could see my cooperation. It felt like an eternity in some strange and tedious purgatory, but it was probably no longer and a couple of minutes at the most. He was just talking and talking, and I remember at some point I had started to play a little game in my head just to see if there were any words at all which sounded remotely familiar to me, out of what he said. But alas, there was not.

After a couple more minutes of this, I recognised his tone lilting up a bit, and then he suddenly fell silent. It was a question. For a split second, I was so proud of myself for being able to recognise anything from his entire speech, even if it was just the tip of the iceberg and not the entire block.

"I guess I need to reply now," I thought to myself as I looked around me for a second. The CEO was smiling at me, his eyebrows raised in an encouraging look as he nodded to me. Others were quietly talking and looking at me, and I am still unsure what it was exactly. At the moment, I didn't even care. I knew I was running out of time, and my brain just froze. I asked myself what would be the smartest thing to do, and my brain responded immediately. Before I could even realise what I had done, my left hand reached out and pushed the button on the big grey device. As the call hung up, I put the receiver back in its place, and then straightened up in my chair.

Though everyone around me seemed confused, this was nothing compared to how I was feeling just then. But I didn't want to look stupid, so I adopted the best serious expression I could find, crossing my fingers under my cheek and looked directly at the CEO like someone who is about to say something really wise.

"That was interesting," I said, finally.

"What did he say?" They all asked me practically at the same time.

"I have no idea," I replied. "I didn't understand a single word he said."

I will never forget the looks on the faces of the people that stood around me. It was similar to the faces that you would find on people right after they had participated in the ice bucket challenge. They were all frozen with shock.

I remember a few hours later when everyone finished with their work for the day and started to go home. I was the only one left working, and as I recalled the events of the day in retrospect, out of the blue, I started to laugh. I thought back to my conversation with the army general, and my laugh became louder and louder until it became hysterical. It took me a few moments to calm myself down before I finally stood up and left. Luckily, enough for me, they have never asked me to speak German ever again.

The Keychain

As we all know, misunderstanding plays a big part in looking silly, and most of the time when people give me a funny look, I figure that someone at some point must have inevitably misunderstood something. And, that is okay, it's just a part of life. Pretty much as certain as death and taxes, am I right? The fact that we all still have this inability to communicate with each other properly, I guess, is one of many, if not the main, reason why we are not yet considered evolved enough to be classified as the perfect species, even though many would probably beg to differ and consider this to be a mark of our higher intellect. I, however, do not.

It is not only a matter of the language barrier or the wrong impressions we get from others. As a matter of fact, the issue most of the time stems from those things that we feel are better left unsaid, rather than being completely honest with one another. And, that in many ways can be a far more dangerous thing than just misunderstanding someone.

When I first started my job in the UK, the Human Resources representative told me that they have a "Clean Desk, Clear Screen" policy. It was something they informed me. We had to take very seriously here, as a committee would frequently and randomly come to check up on everyone. I never thought twice about asking for a more informed opinion. Why would I? You know what they say about the word "assume" and how it can quickly make an ass out of you and me. Well, let's say the man who coined the phrase was more right than he ever knew.

This assumption on my part resulted in me going to my place of work a good bit earlier than everyone else every day for six whole months. I did this to make sure I had plenty of time to come in and clean up my desk with household cleaning products, and clear my computer screen before I would turn it on. I remember after nearly half a year of this habit, one of my colleagues turned up and asked me what I was doing. Of course, I explained to them very confidently that I was cleaning my screen.

"You do that all the time. What's wrong with your screen? Are you eating on it or something?" My co-worker asked.

"No, I just don't want to be caught," I responded.

"Caught by who?" They continued to pry.

"There is a committee which checks up on us randomly," I replied. "They take it very seriously."

After about ten seconds of silence, I saw it cross his face that he finally understood what was going on here, then, burst into obnoxious laughter. He then proceeded to explain to me what the policy meant and that it was referring to data security, and not leaving confidential information lying around on the desk. It is just called "Clean Desk, Clear Screen" policy.

My colleague, after this, of course, called me an idiot and continued laughing at me. If you think about it, I didn't exactly do anything wrong. It was just a big misunderstanding caused by a very big lack of communication, mostly on my part because I didn't bother to ask for an explanation. Like I said before, assume without asking, and you will make an ass out of you and me. I most certainly did in this case, only for it to be remedied by the only way you can fix these sort of things; with proper communication. Even if it does happen to come at the expense of your dignity, and the person who finally clarifies things for you think you are an utter buffoon.

This causes me to remember another point in my life when one of my classmates told me if you don't want to look like an idiot, don't act like one.

For many years I thought he was right to think of me this way. So, I tried to be quiet in school and avoid any situation that could cause me any undue amount of trouble or confrontation. This resulted in the worst years of my life. I was living with the constant fear of not being involved in anything that would make me look foolish or stupid, as well as, a perpetual daily ritual of bowing to the whims of various bullies, all because I was afraid to look like less of a person. In all reality, this only served to lower my self-esteem.

Granted, in certain situations, everyone has acted like an idiot from time to time, and I'm pretty sure it's safe to say not just once. I would even be willing to say that I behave like an idiot, perhaps more than average at times, but I have learned to embrace this and try to see the funny side of it. That's me in a nutshell, and I am happy with myself for the most part as I am. Not to mention, embracing my genius comedic timing has saved my life more than once and got me out of a lot of trouble, too.

For instance, when I was a teenager, I was standing at the bus station one day in the middle of Budapest. Two guys came to me and said something to me. I didn't understand them as they were talking relatively quietly.

"Sorry, what was that?" I said.

They repeated it, and it was definitely something about my wallet, but I still barely understood. So, I just asked them to repeat it again. The funny thing is that it was in the middle of the day and I wasn't the only one standing in the station. So, it didn't appear to be a robbery to me, even though it was very much a robbery, or at least trying to be one.

They told me to give them my phone and my wallet right now looking around to make sure no one was watching.

I was confused because they didn't have a weapon and they didn't even touch me. They were just standing there looking frightened and speaking quietly. So, I slowly reached into my pocket where my phone was located, and I realised I had a keychain with me with several keys on it attached to a lanyard, and it felt pretty heavy. I took it out and slowly started to swing it in the air around me, trying to muster everything I had learned about the kung fu I took for three years when I was little. Needless to say, I was just bullshitting and had no idea what I was doing.

"If you want my wallet, you have to come and get it." I said in my best action movie voice, taking a step backward while swinging the lanyard faster around my head. I eventually tripped backward over something, but recovered, and continued hoping no one noticed.

The keys made a great swishing noise, like helicopter blades, coming closer to my face with every pass. And, it became quickly evident that at some point they were going to hit me square in the face.

I must have looked like some kind of circus clown, ducking with every swipe of the keychain over my head and close to my face. After a little while longer, and hitting myself in the chest, as well as praying that I wouldn't hit myself so hard again, the guys left. They were back as they fled as if they had never seen such an idiot before in their life and they wanted no part of it. That is when I first realised that acting a fool saves me from being robbed.

Suffice it to say, we are all different, and we all react to things differently than one another. So, when I call you weirdo, it only means that you are lucky enough to see the world in a more extraordinary way than others.

I guess the real point I'm trying to make here is that you always remember to live in the present, and learn from your mistakes, as well as embrace the things in yourself that you see as imperfections. For it is these qualities that set you apart from the pack, and one of the greatest gifts in the world.

The Bus

Anyone who has travelled from London to LA, or the other way around, knows how insanely expensive it can be to fly between the two continents. We pretty much spent the majority of our holiday budget on the flight. Therefore we thought we were going to experience the West Coast by renting rooms and small apartments in different places as we travelled around California.

As cheap as I am, I insisted that we take the local bus as frequently as possible to save money, not knowing about the local customs or distances. When we arrived in LA at 1:30 AM, we had our backpacks, a laptop bag, and two pieces of big luggage with us. Laura, my wife, tried to convince me to take a taxi and not carry all of the stuff on the streets. But I assured her that I got used to London, and it couldn't be too much different.

I couldn't have been more wrong. Though my smartphone convinced me that the journey from the airport to the local bus station doesn't take any longer than 20 minutes, 40 minutes later we were still walking deadly close to a construction area, next to the motorway in the dark. The scene pretty much looked like a thriller movie set, but it was much bigger, much closer, and much more real.

I probably should have listened to Laura when she tried to convince me once again to call a cab, but I was determined that we were going to get to the station. Not to mention that I was aware of how much money we could save doing this.

"I'm not gonna spend $50 on a taxi," I said to her. Bus tickets in LA are ridiculously cheap compared to Europe. It took us almost an hour to get to the station, and we had another 10 minutes to wait for the bus. We were both exhausted, but I was stubborn. Suddenly the bus appeared and opened its doors. That's when I realised that night buses in Los Angeles are pretty much used by homeless people. Which also explained why it is so cheap to travel with them.

We hopped on to the bus and kindly asked the driver for tickets. The driver was a huge man, and his face reflected how he felt about our presence, when he almost shouted at me in his west coast accent, "Are you out of your damn mind? What the hell are you looking for here with all of this stuff?"

I found him a bit rude, but I probably was more shocked about his attitude than I let on.

"Excuse me, sir, but what do you mean?" I asked in my strong British accent.

"Where do you wanna go with all of these bags?" He was still shouting.

"To West Hollywood. We should be there in 1.5 hours." I replied.

"Are you aware that you need to change to another bus for that middle way?" He inquired.

"Yes, I am, sir," I said.

"Then, you also know that there is a helluva chance that you're gonna die at that place, right? If someone sees you standing there like a Christmas tree with this bunch of electronics, you bet you're gonna bite the dust." He knowledgeably informed me. Because, it is important to understand that when a person has lived in a place longer than you have, it stands to reason that they would know more about how dangerous it is than you. But because I was too absorbed in my obstinance, I did not think about this and instead remained utterly shocked by the driver's manner, and assured him that we were going to go with this bus whether he liked it or not. Laura seemed to give up her point this time, probably because she was already so embarrassed by my display of ultimate macho stupidity that she found it superfluous to try and reason with someone who has decided to stay so unreasonable. She came to the middle of the bus with me to sit down, in silence. A silence, which all husbands know speaks volumes of its own.

One thing seemed to be right, though, we drew a lot of attention from the people who were on the bus. The strangers looked indeed quite scary, but I tried to focus on the only thing I could think of, how cheap the tickets were, and how much we saved by avoiding the $50 it would cost for a taxi.

We were on the bus for almost an hour, and we almost fell asleep. But I knew that if I did fall asleep, we probably would wake up with a lighter load due to the circumstances. So, I tried to stay focused.

When we got to the point where we had to change for another bus, the driver turned around, looked at us, and warned us one last time, "Are you sure you wanna get off here?"

"Yes, we need to," I replied. "Thank you for the drive," I added, as in the UK it is quite common to thank the driver for the ride when you leave the bus.

We hopped off, and the bus went away in a few seconds. The sound of the vehicle which was fading out slowly reminded me of when you turn off the light in a castle where you spend your night for the first time. For the first time in my life, I was properly scared, even though there was nothing visible to be scared off. It was probably just the scenery, which looked like indeed the worst part of a ghetto. After the bus had gone, there were no other vehicles on the road. It was just us. The whole area smelled terrible. There was graffiti on the walls everywhere there was a wall at all. Some of the houses looked like they had been bombed, parts of the fences were down, and there were some trashed cars at the edge of the sidewalk.

I had goosebumps, and when I looked at Laura, I immediately realised how stupid I was. It's one thing to make stupid decisions when you put yourself at stake. It is a completely different matter to put your loved ones at stake. At that very moment, I felt truly ashamed, and I regret that I was so stubborn. It was too late, though.

"When is the next bus coming?" she asked me.

"In 15 minutes according to the phone."

Suddenly two shapes appeared on the horizon. From the street next to us, the street lamps put some light on the two strangers. One seemed to be a huge man, the other one was, well, it's hard to describe, it was somewhere between a stooping old lady and a giant parrot. Until to this day, I am not entirely sure what we had seen, but it was extraordinary, shocking, and indescribable. They weren't the only ones. In a few seconds, others popped up from different parts of the street, with kerchiefs on their heads, tattoos on their arms, and guns on their belts. I am sure the whole thing happened within few seconds, but it felt like an hour. People just came from the dark, and they all looked at us, approaching our direction. I was still standing there with my camera, laptop bag, and all of other luggage like an idiot. By that point I did not doubt that I would certainly lose everything we had, but what I was most scared for was our lives. It was uncertain what was going to happen now. For a few seconds, I hoped we could blend in, or maybe, them gathering has nothing to do with our presence, maybe they know each other, and usually gather around this time of the night.

That hope quickly disappeared when they started to shout at us, using not too polite comments, and they formed a circle around us. There was no way out of this. I saw Laura crying, and I grabbed her hands strongly.

Now I am sure there are people out there who would describe the following few seconds as luck, others would say it was destiny stepping in, but as we were standing in the middle of the road, surrounded by all these people, suddenly two lights appeared on the horizon. First, I thought it might belong to the gangster-looking people, but they seemed to be confused by the presence of the car. As it got closer, it started to honk, and it had become clear, it was a taxi.

The circle now broke as it wasn't clear if the cab was going to drive on through everyone or go to the sidewalk to avoid the group. It was neither. When it finally got close, it was the biggest surprise to find out that it was doing a drift, like in an action movie, and people almost had to jump out of its way. It was too much to process at that time. I remember I didn't know what was happening. It was so cool and so frightening at the same time. That's why I probably don't remember how we got into the taxi. I remember the driver shouting out something like, "Get in now!" But to be honest, it was mostly Laura who dragged me into the car with every one of our bags, and the next time I had solid memories is from when we were already sitting in the back seat.

The taxi driver didn't say a word for quite long, but he genuinely seemed to be very upset. We went for about 5 minutes without knowing where we were going. At one point, he pulled away and turned around.

"What the hell were you doing out there?" He shouted.

"Wow, in this country, everyone is rude to strangers." I thought. But this time I got the idea why he was angry. Though I couldn't explain myself without being very embarrassed, so I pretty much said it was my fault and the only mine to make that dumb decision. I felt like back in the school after getting a bad grade, explaining it to my mother. The driver asked where we were supposed to be, and then he started the engine.

The journey lasted for about 20 minutes, but we had the chance to have a wonderful view of LA's city from a distance, with its skyscrapers, as they stranded like mountains in the dark. It was truly beautiful. On the radio, there was some jazz playing, and Laura seemed to be calming down slowly, too. Everything felt so surreal, as just a few minutes ago we thought we were going to die.

I apologised to Laura multiple times, and I promised that things like this would never happen again. When we arrived at the address, we got off, I paid a $5 tip to the taxi driver, and even with that we only paid like $35. I was suddenly really happy about it as it was less than I expected.
Laura looked at me after the cab was gone and asked me, "What's the conclusion of this night?"

I suddenly felt the need to highlight one side of the information. "Well, actually we only paid $35, probably because we came a long way with the bus, so we managed to save a bit, which is nice."

I will never forget the look on Laura's face. Because I can say that it scared me more than the whole night put together.

Eric

Whenever you belong to a small nation, and you move to a different place, it is normal to feel like reaching out to others who are from the same area as you are. This usually happens to everyone who has just recently moved to a new country. It also most likely stems from the fact that when you become an immigrant, everything is new to you. The place, the language, the currency, the price of everyday essentials, the different driving regulations; sometimes even what side of the road to drive on. The list could go on and on. You pretty much have to relearn everything you already knew as a part of becoming a functioning member of adult society. So it is completely normal to feel like some kind of an alien outsider in need of connection to someone else around you who shares a common origin as you. This feeling usually fades away with time as you become more accustomed to your new surroundings, and the locals become your mates. Finally, the environment becomes familiar enough to call home.

I was still in that state of a culture shock when I started work for a company as an engineer in England. I was told there was another Hungarian working in the engineering department, and so I looked for him. His name was Thomas, and he was a nice chap. Unfortunately, when I joined, he was already on his notice period, so we only had two weeks to spend any time together during lunch breaks, but still, he was quite a helpful lad who introduced me to how things worked in the company.

On his last day, we said goodbye to each other as he was about to move to a different town for a better job. Our last conversation was interrupted as other colleagues of his came to say goodbye as well. But I clearly remember him telling me to look for Eric, as he was Hungarian too, and he still worked there as well.

I buried that information for about three months, and almost forgot about it. Then one day, I was off to the toilet, when someone shouted in my direction.

"Eric!"

I instantly turned around to see what was going on. It was the guy, standing next to me who they were shouting to. I was standing there as they started a conversation, and I was listening to them completely amazed, with my eyes and mouth wide open. The man who responded had an Eastern European accent. "It's him." I thought.

It took me a moment to realise in my joy that I was standing and listening to them too terribly closely, as I was not a part of the conversation, so after a while, they began to look at me with the kind of face that says, "What the hell are you doing? Why are you spying on us?"

So, I took the hint to go about my own business and continued my way to the toilet, and went straight to the urinal. A few seconds later, another person came and stood next to me in the other urinal. It was Eric. "What do I do now?" I thought. I wanted to start a conversation, where it could be revealed very quickly that we were both from the same country. But I didn't want to push it either and seem creepy, I mean come on, we were already standing in the loo. What could be creepy about a guy suddenly starting a conversation with you in there?

So, I came up with this idea, as we were standing there doing our business, that for some reason at the time I had thought it didn't seem creepy. Even though thinking back on it now, I can only imagine how disturbing I must have appeared.

I thought about when you sigh in Hungary, there is a word you might say while you breathe out loud, which sounds like "Yuuuy." So, it stands to reason that only a Hungarian would know how to use this in the proper context. Hence, I thought this would be the best way to show Eric who I was and where I was from.

As we were still standing at the urinals, I suddenly sighed letting out a huge "yuuy" sound, and then I slowly glanced at Eric. He naturally seemed very confused. So I smiled at him encouragingly and nodded. Nothing happened; he looked away, doing his business. So I thought that he might not have heard me. That's ok. Sometimes you do not encounter a familiar sound for a particular language due to its lack of presence in your environment, so sometimes you simply don't pick up on it right away. I figured this must be the reason for his response.
As I was thinking about this, Eric headed off to wash his hands, so I needed to hurry up if I was going to catch him. I quickly went to the other tap, and while I was washing my hands, I made the sound once again. "Yuuy!"

Eric looked at me again, so I smiled back again, then I slightly nodded in his direction. Once again, thinking back on this, I know I must've looked like one of those child molesters that poses as a candy man, who your parents warn you about on your first day of school. This time Eric seemed to be a bit scared. He froze for a moment awkwardly, before leaving in such a great pace that he didn't even dry his hands. I thought this was a bit odd because if he were Hungarian, he should have reacted to that very differently. So I thought, perhaps, that I would give it a final try later in the kitchen area. But before I did, I needed to check him out on the company's directory online. I found him on the website, and it was clear now that he was not Hungarian at all, but from the eastern part of Romania. I immediately began to mentally kick myself, as I knew that he must think I was a complete imbecile.

Just as I close the browser, it was as if fate had stepped in to lend me a hand. I received an email from the finance department, and the sender was, Erica Martin. The epiphany struck me as it usually does like some sort of lightbulb going off in my head. I had misunderstood Thomas, as he was loudly interrupted by his colleagues during his farewell. It was Erica, not Eric.

I stood up from my desk and went to the stairs to go to the financial department in search of Erica. I went on what seemed a lengthy and arduous quest past many stations. It took what seemed like an eternal trek through some unknown wilderness. I even had to stop and ask a lady in the department where I might find Erica.

Finally, I found her. She was sitting there, from the looks of it she was about eight months pregnant. So I went quite close to her, introduce myself, and ask her, "are you by any chance from Hungary?"

"Yes, I am, why?" She answered.

"Me too!" I exclaimed. Up until this point, I was so excited to meet her, and suddenly I realised there was nothing on earth we could talk about at this point. Also, her face made it very clear that she was not on lunch break yet, might be in the middle of something, and I am definitely the last thing she needs at the moment. It was the wrong time in the wrong place, now that I think back on it. Not to mention, that it was clear that she would soon be off to maternity leave. As I was standing by her sheet, looking like a complete idiot, I started to tell her about the only thing which came to my mind. "Thomas told me to look for you. But I thought you were a man, so I found this Romanian guy, as I thought he was you. But clearly, he isn't." I laughed awkwardly. "it was hilarious because I just followed him to the kitchen. Actually, before that, we were at the toilet, and I thought I was going to say 'yuuy' in front of him, but he didn't understand why I smiled so much on him at the urinals, and I guess he totally freaked out. So, he must be thinking that I am crazy. But now I certainly understand everything. Your real name is Erica, and you are clearly a female, not a man. I am so happy that I finally found you."

She was really shocked. I saw it in her eyes that she has no idea how to react to this and what to think of the words that I just vomited all over her. So you can probably guess that there were a good few seconds where she remained awkwardly silent and glanced back at her colleagues as it is to ask her if this was happening right now. Then, satisfied that she was not hallucinating, or that this was some sort of prank, she went back at me and finally broke her long silence. "Oh, that's quite... interesting. Thanks very much for telling me all of this. It's great that you finally found me."

"Oh, no worries," I responded. "I usually take my lunch break at noon. So, if you ever feel like joining me, just pop along at the engineering department's kitchen."

I still find it fascinating how awkwardly people can behave when they're happy and excited at the same time. At the time, I didn't pay attention to how ridiculously I was acting, but as soon as I told this whole story to my wife Laura, she told me that I should not count on Erica ever joining me for lunch, especially, after this. Laura told me that she, herself, would probably go on maternity leave sooner if she knew that there was a weirdo out there looking for her. I guess it's not that big of a secret to share that she was right, as she usually is, and I never saw Erica ever again.

The Chocolate Cake

When I go to the toilet, I take precautions. I guess by now it's clear with my history why this is important. So when I went to my usual workplace back in the day as a voice actor, I always knew what cabins to avoid with tricky flushing handles, what taps are the ones that have the strongest water pressure, and when to go to the toilets to avoid a traffic jam.

I know it's strange for Americans, but here in Europe we have these toilets at random places where the inner porcelain forms a tray inside of the toilet, so the poo doesn't go to the water immediately but to the tray, where the water will flush it down when needed. Why it's like that, I have no idea. It might give an opportunity for people to take a look at what they have produced before flushing the content on the tray down, but other than this, I really can't tell what it is good for.

This workplace happened to have this kind of toilet trays, but I never had a problem with them. I can already hear you saying to yourself, "Until now."

I like to imagine in my head the young Chris as a blockbuster movie protagonist. A secret agent who takes every toilet going as a mission, avoiding people, playing with the timing, waiting at the corridor, blending in. And for many years it worked perfectly well. I arrived at the building, signed in as a worker for the day, got my white plastic magnet card for the whole day to open the studio doors, and then I disappeared from the curious eyes. The soundtrack to every spy movie ever made playing in my subconscious as I pictured myself to be the James Bond of going to the loo, in private.

However, it so happened that once I felt the need to go to the toilet just before I started work. There was nothing unusual about this. Everything went according to plan. And, I was ready to deal with the paperwork, then leave for the day. The only thing I did not anticipate was that even a super-secret agent could make mistakes sometimes.

You see, I had placed my magnet card in my hip pocket, and when I looked into the toilet after getting up from doing my business, I noticed something very interesting waiting for me inside the toilet indeed. It looked like a chocolate cake, where all the paper was covering the sides like frosting on a cake, and on top there appeared to be a birthday card. "What the hell?" I thought to myself before I realised that it was my plastic card sticking out of the pile of poo.

"What the hell do I do now?" A question which I ask myself so many times, that by this point in my life it has become my mantra.

The worst thing about fumbling through your shit is not the fact that whatever is stuck in it is going to slowly sink more and more into it like quicksand. It's not even the fact that the object will need to be cleaned, and that's just disgusting to think about. The real problem is that whatever has been stuck in the pile of shit is going to stink, much like a corpse that has been left out in the sun for too long. And, there is quite literally nothing you can do about it. I wiped the card and washed it thoroughly in the sink. I was sure to use hand soap many times over, but still, the card smelled like shit. Unfortunately, I was not the only one who thought this.

      A few moments passed when I was back in the studio with Amanda, another teenager as we were doing voice over for movie scenes together. We had worked together for years and knew each other quite well. Though, of course, she had absolutely no idea about my history with toilets. After a while, I noticed that she was looking around suspiciously, until one point she finally asked me, "Do you smell that, too?"

"What are you talking about?" I tried to play dumb.

"Something smells like shit." She explained.

"What's wrong guys?" The sound director spoke to us using the mic which connected to the speakers found inside of our soundproof booth.

"I don't know," I responded.

"Sorry, it's just--" Amanda shook her head. "Something stinks in here."

"I don't smell anything. It might be my perfume that you're smelling." I came back with the worst possible line ever.

"Why? Does your perfume smell like shit?" She retorted with her best teenager's canny, unspoken manner.

"That's a good point," I thought. "Hopefully not," I didn't sound too convincing this time.

"Do you want me to come in?" Asked the director, who now was becoming a bit anxious about the unplanned delay.

"Nah, we're good," I said, as the glorious solution suddenly reached my mind as if it were a gift from heaven. "I am sure someone just stepped in some dog shit out there."

"Ah, that's possible." Amanda agreed and immediately checked her shoes.

I realised I had to do the same, and I tried to do so at such an angle where she couldn't look at my clean shoe soles.

"Yep, you were right," I said. "It's on me. I stepped in the dog poo."

"Then, take them off, give them to me, and I throw them out of the booth." She ordered.

I looked at her in shock. There was no way I was going to give her my shoes. If she realised that they were clean, she could have found out that it was me that smelled like shit. I mean the card. You know what I mean.

"It's not necessary," I said. "I can take care of it."

So I proceeded to leave the booth for a moment, I took my completely clean shoes, and then I removed my card from my pocket, and placed it into my shoes; thinking to myself, "Great, now I will have to throw my shoes out after this."

Once the offensive object had been removed from the booth, everyone seemed to calm down, and we went on with our work as we would normally, finishing the rest of the day without incident, or any more unnecessary shit.

Moral of the story, when in doubt, if there is something smelly and you know that it is you, blame it on a phantom dog. Also, the one who smelled it is the one who dealt it and don't be afraid to let the person who smells it first understand that it is the guilty dog who barks first.

The Airplane

Several years before becoming an engineer and moving to the UK, I accepted jobs from all over the world as a performer. I performed all over Europe, and not just as an actor, but occasionally also as a dancer or a presenter, depending on the nature of the project. That's partly because I love travelling, and learning new languages, but I also can't deny that the salaries in the West are much better compared to the Eastern European market.

One time a very interesting role was offered to me. I had to be the Master of Ceremony at an event where Baroque Opera pieces were presented in England. That was the very first time I started to work on my British Accent, even though the Opera Festival's organiser assured me that the pronunciation is not that important for them, but the comical personality is. So I took the job, and they flew me off to London in a few weeks along with some of the best musicians of Hungary. And when I say some of the best, I say it for a reason. They were not just teaching at the Academy of Music in Budapest, they also won awards and had the chance to play in symphonic orchestras, which are the most respected ones in the world. Having the chance to work with them was mind-blowing to me as someone who has such a great interest in music. That's why our journey back to Budapest is so very hard to describe without appearing uncivilized.

Back in the days when you were travelling with particular

low-budget airlines, you couldn't buy seats, you just showed up, queued up as quick as possible, and you took the seat with your travelling mates which you fancied the most. For many years that's how everyone was travelling who didn't want to spend much more for tickets with fancy airlines.

Therefore when we queued up with the musicians to our plane, we knew we had to stay in the queue for at least an hour before they allowed us to step on-board. That's a long time if you have to pee. That's even longer if you have to poo. But when you feel you've got food poisoning and going to have the worst diarrhoea, that feels like eternity. You may ask, why didn't I ask someone to reserve my place, and the response to that comes from the fact that we were told many times by the flight attendants that the gates were about to open within 5 minutes. And then they delayed it. Again. And again.

  I felt like I'd need at least 20 minutes reserved at the toilet so I thought all I have to do is to wait until we can step aboard, and then I'll run off to the toilets, and no one will force me out until we land in Budapest.

  This, however, was a terrible plan. What I didn't know was that once we stepped on board, we had to go take our seats and they said I couldn't go to the toilet before reaching the travelling latitude. So I sat down in the middle of the row between two female musicians, and I closed my eyes. It took another 20 minutes until we finally took off, and after a point, I felt I was going to explode here, and it's going to be the most disgusting explosion ever on a plane in human history. I was trying to meditate, but I was sweating, and I couldn't focus on my breathing and relax without risking shitting myself. I had to stay tight, so the gates of hell would stay closed.

When the plane has finally departed from the ground, everyone was forced into their seats, and the gate was just about to be opened. I needed all of my meditational skills to focus on my glutes and all the years of ballet practice, which was at that moment counted as a multi-year training for this very moment.

As the automated sound finally was triggered by the captain to show that we could release the belts now, I jumped out from the row like a gazelle on the Savannah. My small backpack was on my right shoulder just in case there is no tissue inside, and I was so determined and quick that no one could be quicker.

I finally went into the extra mini toilet room with the oblique ceiling. And, I am not kidding when I say, in a few minutes, I had rebuilt the darker, and smaller version of the Great Pyramid of Giza. The amount of stuff coming out of me was so abundant that it's hard to describe it properly. I could if I wanted to, but I am not sure if it is worth the effort. But the point is that I finally was rescued and relieved. I stayed there for a few minutes to make sure I was going to be all right now when suddenly there was an automated sound again, and then the captain said something very long and then all went silent.

It was another minute or so before someone came knocking on the door. It was the flight attendant, she was saying something

That's Life

about turbulence, and that I had to come out from the toilet.

"Well that's not the best idea," I thought to keep in mind that I haven't flushed yet and I knew it was gonna take a while before all of the waste went down the toilet.

I waited silently, and then they knocked again. And then finally everything went completely silent. It was almost calming. Just the loud noise the plane generated, and nothing else. No chit-chat from other passengers, no shouting from flight attendants, just the loud humming noise, and me.

"Alright, time to go." I thought, and I started to reach for the toilet paper on the wall.

The next few moments are very blurry, but what I realised retrospectively is that the plane must have descended a few meters within a second. That resulted me into basically flying to the solid, oblique ceiling, hitting my head very hard, and then ending up in a twisted squat posture on the ground, hitting my head again against the wall of this incredibly small space.

I must have been there for a few seconds before I realised what was going on. Everything was much darker and blurrier. The first thing I noticed was the smell.

"What's this?" I thought before looking up.

That was the moment when I realised that it wasn't just me who jumped up high. It was the pyramid too, extracted and re-formed in a much more disgusting way. The small room's landscape had been totally changed. I could say it was the fifty shades of brown. Where there was a mirror before, it literally wasn't clear anymore what was there. The toilet itself wasn't empty, but it was definitely less occupied than earlier as most of the stuff had flown out. And that wasn't everything. My shit might have covered the tiny walls and the mirror, but it made no exception with me.

As much as I could tell, I was pretty much covered with my fluid and faeces in random places.

It was a stinky, moving hell, miles above the ground. And there was no one there to tell me what to do now.

    As I pulled myself together, I realised I needed to do something with this place. It was clear I could not clean up everything, but I needed to try at least a bit so I wouldn't smell like shit when I got back to my seat. I was lucky enough to have my small backpack with me as it was full of tissues. I started to clear the mirror, and then myself. And then I pulled out my deodorant and used the whole bottle in a matter of 30 seconds. So far, the air was shitty, but I could breathe. From this moment, as the smell mixed with the fragrance, I couldn't even breathe anymore. I thought I was going to die in that place. It was literally the worst death I could ever have imagined to myself.

    I must have spent at least 10 minutes in the toilet, trying to clean up everything, but I only got to the point where all the toilet paper and tissues made the loo full. It was time to flush. Or so I thought.

I pushed the button, but nothing happened. I tried again, and again, and again.

Suddenly I realised there is a paper printed on the wall which was hard to read because it was pretty much fully covered with my shit, so I had to take some additional tissues from my bag to wipe it off. Speaking of pyramids, I felt like someone from ancient Egypt who just discovered some holy texts on the wall and needed to wipe off the dust to be able to read it.

My face was full of interest as I was about to discover something. It was a sign which basically warned not to put any toilet papers into the loo as it will block the flush.
Up to this moment, I could pull myself together. But then I looked at myself, then at the wiped mirror, and started to cry. I looked like someone who just got back from a war and lost his family. In reality, of course, it wasn't that bad, I just basically managed to break an airplane's toilet and put it into a state where probably no one ever would be able to use it again. I wondered at that moment that the damage must have been so bad that they essentially would need to replace the whole plastic room with a new one.

I gave myself another minute or so, and then I left the room. No one was there. Everyone was sitting silently. The aisles were dark, and only some signal lights were left on. It seemed all calmed and relaxed. For a second, it was almost like a ghost plane. Since there were no flight attendants around, I decided to leave things like that, and I double-checked if my deo fragrance was still stronger than the smell of my shit. I couldn't tell, but to be honest, at that point I didn't care too much. All I cared was that no staff member would be angry with me, for what happened during the turbulence.

When I sat back in my place, the musicians were sleeping, so I had nothing to be scared of. The journey was like 1.5 hours left, so I put some music on from my phone, and tried to sleep a bit too. In reality, I was reliving the whole scene over and over again in my head and tried to figure out why these things were only happening to me, and not to any of my friends.

When we took off, I saw the toilet from the outside again as we passed next to it, this time it was closed down with some plastic ribbons, similar to what the police use to close down criminal venues. I didn't blame them; for me, it was completely understandable. I was wondering if there would be any consequences as we were about to leave the airport. Do they have footage of me going in and going out? Will they at some point come for me, and put me in jail? I didn't want to be on the news for shitting all over the plane.

For my biggest relief, though there wasn't. We left the airport, and I decided to bury this whole story deep down, and never talk about it again.

Apparently, I fail in everything.

ABOUT THE AUTHOR

Chris is a writer and engineer, well-known for his sense of humour. Originally from Hungary, he moved to the UK to pursue engineering after working as a musical and voice actor.

Printed in Poland
by Amazon Fulfillment
Poland Sp. z o.o., Wrocław